HOW TO MAKE SOULFUL CONNECTIONS

AWAKENING THE MAGIC OF TRUE CONNECTION IN EVERY INTERACTION

REV RANJI VARUGHIS

Made with ♥ on the Notion Press Platform
www.notionpress.com

Contents

Contents

Introduction

Have you ever wondered what it truly means to connect with another human being? To delve into the depths of their soul, unraveling the intricacies of their thoughts and emotions, and building a bond that withstands the test of time? If so, then you have come to the right place, my dear reader.

Welcome to the enchanted world of How to make Soulful Connections. Within the pages of this book, I invite you on a transformative journey that will empower you to forge authentic bonds with those around you. Prepare yourself, for we are about to embark on a remarkable adventure that will forever change the way you perceive and navigate the realm of human connections.

As we gather here, let me tell you a little about myself. Rev Ranji Varughis, at your service. A humble Christian Priest, Counsellor and Chaplain who has been blessed with the opportunity to work with individuals from all walks of life. From bright-eyed students eager to uncover their passions to weary souls searching for solace amidst life's storms, my experiences have taught me the true value of genuine relationships.

Picture, if you will, a vibrant tapestry woven with threads of laughter, tears, and the inexplicable magic of human connection. Each stitch meticulously crafted, forming an intricate pattern of understanding, empathy, and shared experiences. This tapestry holds the key to unlocking a world where relationships are not merely superficial interactions, but rather, they become a kaleidoscope of emotions that enrich our lives.

At the very heart of Soulful Connections lies the timeless wisdom that it is through our connections that we experience the profound beauty of life. We will explore the power of vulnerability, decipher the language of emotions, and learn to cultivate meaningful relationships in both our personal and professional spheres. By delving deep into the essence of human connections, we will uncover the secrets to building bonds that transcend superficiality, nurturing them into something truly extraordinary.

With tranquil prose and gentle pacing, we will traverse through the enchanting chapters of this book. Each page will envelop you in a world filled with soft, sensory imagery and the soothing embrace of heartfelt stories. Together, we will embark on a journey that offers not only practical advice, but also the touch of simplicity needed to navigate the complexities of building genuine relationships.

As the sun sets on the horizon, casting hues of golden warmth upon the world, we will learn to appreciate the beauty of connection. From the laughter-filled gatherings with friends to the tender moments shared with loved ones, Soulful Connections will gift you with the tools to foster bonds that are both meaningful and endearing.

Open your heart and mind, my dear reader, as we transcend the barriers of superficiality and delve into the depth of human connection. Are you ready to embark on this remarkable adventure? To unravel the mysteries of the human soul and build relationships that stand the test of time? If so, then join me on this extraordinary journey through the pages of Soulful Connections: The Art of Building Genuine Relationships. Together, let us discover the true essence of what it means to connect – in a way that will forever change the tapestry of our lives.

Foreshadow

As I sit here, pen in hand, I am reminded of the immense power that lies within the intricate webs of human connections. It is in the delicate dance of emotions, the exchange of hearts, and the intertwining of souls that we find the true essence of who we are and what it truly means to be alive. In a world where superficiality has become the norm, where screens have replaced faces and emojis have replaced emotions, the art of building genuine relationships has been cast aside, like a forgotten masterpiece hidden away in the depths of a darkened gallery. But fear not, for within the pages of this book, a transformative guide awaits, ready to breathe life back into the art of connection.

Broad Overview:
"How to make Soulful Connections", is an enchanting journey that beckons forth the beauty and magic of human connection. Through insightful wisdom and practical advice, I will empower you, dear reader, to forge bonds that transcend the superficial and embrace the authentic. From personal to professional spheres, from friendships to romances, this book unlocks the secrets of creating relationships that are not only meaningful but also enduring.

Highlight Key Sections or Chapters:
Within the pages of this book, each chapter acts as a portal to an alternate universe, where the power of authenticity, active listening, trust, and emotional intimacy take center stage. We will explore the delicate dance of setting boundaries and practicing self-care, the transformative

effects of empathy and compassion, as well as the art of navigating differences and conflicts with grace and understanding. Together, we will uncover the transformative effects of gratitude and appreciation, and learn to sustain and nurture soulful connections over time. We will delve into the magic of small gestures and the joy of shared experiences, and embrace the art of mindful communication as a means to foster understanding, empathy, and harmony within our relationships.

Outline Learning Objectives:
By the end of this book, not only will you possess a wealth of knowledge about the intricacies of genuine connection, but you will also have gained practical insights and strategies to implement in your own life. You will become adept at nurturing and preserving meaningful relationships, and will have a newfound understanding of the profound impact that such connections can have on your overall well-being. Through this journey, you will discover the transformative power of human connection and its ability to shape the course of our lives.

Personal Relevance:
Dear reader, I invite you to reflect upon your own life as you embark on this remarkable adventure. Recall the cherished relationships that have enriched your existence and ponder the depths to which you yearn to cultivate new connections. Whether you are a young adult navigating the turbulent waters of college life or a seasoned professional seeking to deepen your personal connections, the wisdom woven within these pages will resonate with you on a soulful level. For it is through genuine relationships that we find solace, inspiration, and the shared experiences that

bring meaning to our lives.

Provide Assurance:
Navigating the complexities of human connection can sometimes feel overwhelming, leaving us adrift in a sea of uncertainty. Yet, I assure you, dear reader, that this book seeks to light your path amidst the darkness, to guide you through the winding corridors of connection with grace and understanding. Together, we will illuminate the mysteries that shroud our interactions and unveil the essence of what it truly means to forge genuine relationships.

End with a Call to Engagement:
And so, dear reader, I extend my hand to you, inviting you to enter this realm of discovery, growth, and transformation. Be prepared to redefine the way you connect with others and to cultivate bonds that transcend the superficial. With an open heart and an open mind, let us embark on this extraordinary journey through the pages of "How to make Soulful Connections." Together, let us unravel the mysteries of the human soul and create a tapestry of connections that will forever enrich our lives.

CHAPTER I

The Power of Authenticity

Embracing Your True Self

The journey of self-discovery is not a linear path but rather a winding road filled with twists and turns, peaks and valleys. It requires a willingness to delve deep within ourselves, confronting our fears, insecurities, and past traumas. This introspective journey can be both exhilarating and daunting, as we uncover hidden layers of ourselves that have been buried beneath the surface.

One approach to self-discovery is through reflection and meditation. Taking the time to sit in silence and listen to the whispers of our soul can reveal profound insights about who we are at our core. Through guided introspection, we can ask ourselves probing questions that unravel our true desires, values, and passions. In doing so, we begin to see the difference between the expectations society has placed upon us and our unique, authentic selves.

Self-acceptance is an integral part of embracing our true selves. It involves recognizing our strengths and weaknesses, accepting our flaws, and forgiving ourselves for past mistakes. It is a process of embracing the totality of who we are, including both our light and shadow selves. When we accept ourselves unconditionally, we cultivate a deep sense of self-worth and authenticity, which radiates in our relationships with others.

Authentic relationships are built upon the foundation of self-acceptance and self-love. When we operate from a place of authenticity, we attract like-minded individuals who see us for who we truly are. These connections are grounded in trust, transparency, and vulnerability, as both parties feel safe to express their true thoughts, emotions, and desires. Such relationships provide us with a sense of belonging, acceptance, and support.

However, embracing our true selves and building authentic relationships does not mean we will never face challenges or conflicts. Quite the contrary, it is in the realm of authenticity that true growth and transformation occur. The willingness to show up as our true selves, even when it feels uncomfortable, allows us to navigate through conflicts with integrity and honesty. It gives us the courage to communicate our needs and boundaries, fostering deeper understanding and connection with others.

In conclusion, exploring the journey of self-discovery and self-acceptance is a vital step toward building genuine connections with others. It requires us to peel back the layers of societal conditioning and embrace our true, authentic selves. By doing so, we create a solid foundation for relationships grounded in trust, vulnerability, and authenticity. It is through these soulful connections that we truly thrive and experience the depth of human connection.

The Art of Vulnerability

There is a remarkable beauty that lies within vulnerability, a beauty that transcends our fear of being seen and allows us to establish deep connections with others. As an experienced Christian priest and counselor who has worked with school and college students, as well as people going through crises, I have witnessed firsthand the transformative power of vulnerability in building genuine relationships.

Vulnerability, often misconstrued as weakness, is far from it. In fact, it takes tremendous strength and courage to open ourselves up to the possibility of being hurt or rejected. It requires a willingness to let others into the depths of our being, exposing our fears, insecurities, and shortcomings. When we dare to be vulnerable, we allow ourselves to be seen for who we truly are.

Let me share with you a story that exemplifies the beauty and strength found in vulnerability. During my counseling sessions, I encountered a young woman named Sarah who had experienced a devastating loss in her life. She had lost her mother unexpectedly, which shattered her sense of security and left her feeling numb. Sarah carried the weight of her grief within, unable to express her pain or seek solace from others. But as we gradually built a trusting relationship, Sarah found the courage to let her guard down and embrace vulnerability.

In our sessions, Sarah began to open up about her deepest emotions and fears. She spoke of her longing to feel connected to others but revealed her hesitance to fully trust again after experiencing such immense loss. As she unveiled the layers of her pain and allowed herself to be seen in her vulnerability, a remarkable transformation occurred. Sarah discovered that her willingness to be vulnerable and to share her pain with others created a space for healing and connection.

What Sarah initially feared as weakness became her greatest strength. In sharing her struggles with vulnerability, she found solace in the empathetic hearts of those around her. Through their support, Sarah realized that vulnerability is the key to authentic connections. By opening up and allowing others to bear witness to her pain, she found comfort, understanding, and ultimately, a renewed sense of hope.

Research on vulnerability supports these findings. Renowned vulnerability researcher Brené Brown discovered that vulnerability is the birthplace of love, belonging, joy, courage, and creativity in our lives. She emphasizes the importance of embracing vulnerability as the path to wholehearted living and genuine connections. When we are willing to lower our walls, we create an opportunity for others to do the same, fostering deep connections built on trust and understanding.

So how can we unlock the art of vulnerability in our own lives? It starts with embracing our imperfections and acknowledging that we are all a work in progress. When we let go of the need to appear perfect or invulnerable, we allow ourselves the freedom to be authentic. Vulnerability is about deeply connecting with others by revealing our true selves, including the messy and imperfect parts.

In our increasingly disconnected and fragmented world, vulnerability is the antidote. By actively practicing vulnerability in our relationships, we open the door for genuine human connection to flourish. When we dare to be vulnerable, we create a safe space where others feel seen, heard, and valued.

In the following chapters, we will explore various exercises and practices that will help you cultivate vulnerability in your own life and unlock its transformative power. Together, we will dive deeper into the art of vulnerability, learning how to navigate the delicate balance between openness and self-preservation, and discovering the immense value vulnerability brings to our relationships.

I invite you to join me on this journey of unveiling the beauty and strength found in vulnerability. Let us embrace our authentic selves and forge genuine connections built on trust, empathy, and love.

Overcoming Fear of Rejection

Throughout my experience working with students, young adults, and individuals going through crisis, I have observed the devastating effects of the fear of rejection. It hinders our ability to be vulnerable, to put ourselves out there, and to open our hearts to others. However, I firmly believe that anyone can conquer this fear and form profound connections with the right guidance and tools.

Now, let me guide you step by step on how to overcome the fear of rejection and embrace the potential of meaningful connections:

Step 1: Understand the Root of the Fear

Before we can conquer any fear, it is essential to comprehend its origin. The fear of rejection often stems from past experiences of abandonment, mistreatment, or neglect. It can be influenced by childhood traumas, unhealthy relationships, or social anxieties. By recognizing and acknowledging the root cause of our fear, we can begin to unravel its grip on us. Once we have unravelled the grip of fear and understand its origin, we are armed with the power to conquer it. But how do we go about this daunting task? The answer lies in introspection, self-reflection, and a willingness to face our past head-on.

To begin, it is imperative to create a safe space for ourselves – both physically and emotionally. This sanctuary will serve as a refuge where we can dive deep into the depths of our psyche and confront the ghostly echoes of past traumas. Only in this sacred space can we truly begin to unravel the intricate layers of our fears.

With pen in hand and an open heart, we embark on a journey of self-discovery. We write down every memory, every emotion, and every thought that has contributed to our fear of rejection. Through this process, we confront the painful experiences that have molded our understanding of rejection. We allow ourselves to grieve for the wounds inflicted upon us and validate the pain we have endured.

Yet, we must not dwell solely on the past. As we navigate through our written confessions, we begin to acknowledge the patterns and behaviors that perpetuate our fear. We examine the internal narratives we have crafted, the beliefs we hold about ourselves, and the expectations we place on others. It is in this introspection that we can identify the distorted perceptions that keep us trapped in the clutches of rejection.

In tandem with our self-reflection, seeking therapy or guidance from a compassionate professional can be transformative. Through their lens, we gain fresh insights and perspectives. A skilled therapist can help us challenge the distorted thoughts, untangle the emotional knots, and guide us towards an empowered understanding of ourselves.

Equipped with newfound self-awareness and armed with professional guidance, we must now confront our fear in real life situations. This is where our courage is truly tested. We expose ourselves to the possibility of rejection, knowing that growth and resilience lie on the other side of our comfort zone.

We take small steps, gradually pushing ourselves further out of our familiar boundaries. We engage in social interactions, initiate conversations, and pursue opportunities that once seemed insurmountable. And yes, there may be moments where rejection stings, where old wounds are prodded, and where tears may be shed. But with each experience, we become better equipped to face our fears head-on.

Along this arduous path, it is crucial to practice self-compassion. We must remind ourselves that conquering fear is not a linear journey, but a winding road filled with peaks and valleys. We must be patient and gentle with ourselves, celebrating every step forward, no matter how small. And when setbacks occur, as they inevitably will, we must resist the urge to berate ourselves, recognizing that setbacks do not define our ability to overcome.

As we persevere, something remarkable begins to happen. The fear that once held us captive dwindles in strength, gradually replaced by newfound courage and resilience. We start to feel a sense of liberation, as the weight of fear lifts from our shoulders. With each fear conquered, we emerge stronger, wiser, and more attuned to our authentic selves.

So, dear reader, be not discouraged by the daunting task ahead. With introspection, professional guidance, and unwavering determination, you have the power to conquer the fear of rejection. Embrace this journey with open arms, for the rewards of self-discovery and personal growth await you on the other side. And remember, the greatest triumph lies not in the absence of fear, but in the courage to confront it and transcend its grasp.

Step 2: Challenge Negative Thought Patterns

Once we have identified the source of your fear, it is time to challenge the negative thought patterns that perpetuate it. Our minds have a remarkable ability to create stories that reinforce our insecurities and doubts. These stories often manifest as self-critical thoughts, leading us to believe that we are not deserving of love or acceptance. However, the truth is far from that. We are all inherently deserving of love and acceptance just as we are. It is vital to recognize that the negative thought patterns we have developed over time are learned behaviors, and just like any learned behavior, they can be unlearned.

To challenge these harmful thought patterns, we must first bring awareness to them. Take a moment to observe the negative thoughts that arise when you feel fear or doubt. Write them down or speak them aloud, acknowledging their presence but not allowing them to define you.

Next, it is essential to question the validity of these thoughts. Ask yourself: What evidence do I have to support this thought? Is this thought a distortion or an exaggeration? Often, we find that these negative thoughts are baseless assumptions, not grounded in reality.

Once you have identified the invalidity of the negative thoughts, it is time to reframe them. Replace those self-critical thoughts with positive and empowering ones. For every negative thought that arises, find evidence to contradict it. Affirmations can be powerful tools in this process. Repeat affirmations such as, "I am worthy of love and acceptance," "I am deserving of happiness," or "I am enough just as I am." These statements help rewire your mind to focus on self-compassion and self-acceptance.

Additionally, seek out support from loved ones or professionals who can help you challenge these negative thought patterns. Surround yourself with people who believe in your inherent worth and are willing to remind you of it when you need it most.

Remember, challenging negative thought patterns takes time and practice. Be patient and gentle with yourself throughout this process. Celebrate even the smallest victories and acknowledge the progress you are making. Trust that as you persist in challenging these thoughts, you will create new stories that support and empower you.

In time, you will realize that the stories your mind weaves can be rewritten. You are the author of your own narrative, and you have the power to shape it into one of self-love, acceptance, and resilience. Embrace this journey of self-discovery, and let it be the catalyst for a profound transformation within you.

Step 3: Cultivate Authenticity and Vulnerability

Authenticity and vulnerability are the foundations of genuine connections. However, the fear of rejection often compels us to wear masks and project an image that we believe will protect us from potential harm. Yet, by doing so, we inadvertently distance ourselves from experiencing true intimacy. In a world obsessed with perfection and filtered realities, it becomes increasingly rare to find genuine connections based on authenticity and vulnerability. Society teaches us to put on a facade, to mask our true selves in order to fit into predefined molds and avoid judgment. The fear of rejection looms over us, haunting our every decision, causing us to hide behind a carefully constructed image.

We convince ourselves that by projecting this idealized version of ourselves, we will shield our delicate hearts from potential harm. We become masters at hiding our insecurities, burying our true thoughts and emotions deep within the recesses of our souls. But what we fail to realize is that these masks only serve to distance us further from the profound connections we yearn for.

Our fear of rejection blinds us to the fact that vulnerability is a strength, not a weakness. Opening ourselves up to another individual requires an immense amount of courage, but it is this very act that provides the foundation for genuine intimacy. When we allow ourselves to be vulnerable, when we remove the layers of protection we've meticulously woven, we create space for a deep and meaningful connection to flourish.

Embracing authenticity is not an easy task, for it requires us to confront our innermost fears and insecurities. It involves dismantling the walls we've built around ourselves and choosing to be unapologetically true to who we are. It demands that we release the need for validation from others and instead seek solace in the acceptance of ourselves.

By shedding our masks, we invite others to do the same. We create a safe haven where trust and mutual understanding can thrive. In sharing our authentic selves, we inspire those around us to be genuine, to let go of pretenses and embrace their own uniqueness.

True intimacy is born in these vulnerable moments. Walls crumble, revealing raw emotions and honest intentions. In this sacred space, we find solace in the warmth of another's embrace, knowing that they have seen the real us, flaws and all, and have chosen to stay.

Through authenticity and vulnerability, we lay the groundwork for connections that transcend superficiality. We embark on a journey of discovering the depth and richness of another's soul, and in turn, they learn the intricacies and beauty of ours. We become intertwined, bound by the understanding that our scars, our imperfections, are what make us whole and deserving of love.

So let us cast aside the masks we wear and embrace the vulnerability that lies within us all. Let us embrace our authentic selves and step into the light of true intimacy. For it is in these moments of connection and rawness that we find the fulfillment we have always longed for.

Step 4: Develop Resilience

Even with the most profound personal growth and deconstruction of fear, rejection may still arise from time to time. Therefore, it is essential to develop resilience and the tools to bounce back when faced with rejection. In a world that often tests the mettle of even the strongest souls, learning to navigate the tumultuous waters of rejection becomes paramount. It is a skill that separates the resilient few from the disheartened many. Rejection, like a bitter pill, can bring an initial wave of sadness and self-doubt, threatening to drown even the most buoyant spirits. But it is precisely in these moments of adversity that the seeds of personal growth are sown.

To develop true resilience, one must practice the art of self-reflection. Instead of wallowing in self-pity, take a step back when faced with rejection and ask yourself: What can I learn from this experience? Was there something I could have done differently? Self-awareness is the key that unlocks the door to growth, allowing you to see opportunity in every setback.

Furthermore, cultivating a sense of perseverance can be an invaluable asset when confronted with rejection. The path to success is rarely a straightforward one, and setbacks are inevitable. Embracing failure as an integral part of the journey will help flip rejection on its head, transforming it into motivation rather than defeat. Keep moving forward, even in the face of adversity, for persistence is the secret weapon that allows dreams to flourish.

Another vital tool in navigating the treacherous terrain of rejection is the power of positive thinking. It may sound cliché, but optimism carries tremendous weight when faced with disappointment. It is the light that pierces through the clouded darkness and provides hope for a brighter future. Look for the silver linings in every rejection, for they exist, even if hidden beneath layers of disappointment. Train your mind to see the lessons and opportunities that accompany failure, enabling you to bounce back stronger than ever before.

Moreover, surround yourself with a supportive network of like-minded individuals who believe in your potential. Seek out mentors, friends, and family members who will uplift and encourage you during times of rejection. Their unwavering support can fuel the fire within, reigniting the spark of self-belief that may momentarily waver. Remember that rejection is not a reflection of your worth, but rather an indication that you are daring to dream beyond the limits of your comfort zone.

Lastly, never underestimate the power of perseverance and patience. Rome was not built in a day, and neither are dreams realized overnight. Rejection can feel like an insurmountable obstacle, but it is merely a stepping stone on the path to success. Embrace the journey, relishing in the challenges that shape and mold you into the resilient individual you are destined to become.

In conclusion, rejection, although painful, can be an opportunity for growth and transformation. Rise above the bitterness that rejection may bring and strive to develop your resilience. Use self-reflection, perseverance, positive thinking, a supportive network, and unwavering patience as your guiding compasses in the face of rejection. Embody the spirit of a true warrior, unafraid to face setbacks and learning to bounce back with grace and determination. For it is through these trials that the indomitable human spirit is forged, ready to conquer any obstacle that stands in the way of greatness.

Step 5: Embrace the Possibility of Meaningful Connections

Armed with a deeper understanding of your fear, self-acceptance, authentic vulnerability, and resilience, you are now ready to embrace the possibility of meaningful connections without the heavy burden of fear. You stand at the precipice of a new chapter in your life, filled with hope and anticipation. The journey toward embracing meaningful connections without the weight of fear has not been easy, but you have emerged stronger, wiser, and more compassionate.

As you step forward into this uncharted territory, remember to be gentle with yourself. Recognize that vulnerability is not a weakness but a courageous act of opening your heart to the world. It is through these authentic moments of vulnerability that true connections can be forged.

Allow yourself to be seen, truly seen, by others. Let them witness your hopes, dreams, and insecurities without the fear of judgment. Understand that not everyone will reciprocate this vulnerability, but those who do will meet you with genuine empathy, compassion, and understanding.

Trust, though scarred from past disappointments, will become your steadfast companion. It will be the foundation upon which deep connections are built. But trust is a delicate balance, requiring both discernment and faith. Follow your intuition, listen to the whisperings of your heart, and trust that it will guide you towards those who are deserving of your vulnerability.

Resilience will also be your closest ally throughout this journey. It will armor you against the potential heartaches and disappointments that come with forging meaningful connections. Understand that not every interaction will result in a lasting bond, but with resilience, you will bounce back stronger each time.

Embrace the richness of human connection in all its forms. Seek out diverse perspectives and engage in meaningful conversations that broaden your horizons. Be open to the possibility that your deepest connections may come from unexpected sources.

Remember, too, to be mindful of your fears, for they may linger in the shadows, waiting to resurface. But armed with the understanding you have gained, you have the power to navigate through them. Acknowledge them with compassion, but do not allow them to define your path or hinder your growth.

As you embark on this journey toward meaningful connections, celebrate the beauty that lies within each encounter. Cherish the moments of laughter, shared tears, and mutual growth. Embrace the diverse tapestry of human connection that weaves its way through your life.

And above all, remain true to yourself. Let the liberation of self-acceptance be the guiding light that illuminates your path. Your unique essence is what makes you irreplaceable, and it is in embracing this truth that you will attract connections that nourish your soul.

Armed with deeper understanding, self-acceptance, authentic vulnerability, and resilience, you navigate the vast sea of human connection. As you sail forth, remember that the potential for meaningful connections is boundless, awaiting your embrace.

Remember, overcoming the fear of rejection is a deeply personal process, and it may take time. But with patience, self-compassion, and the tools provided in this book, you will gradually free yourself from the shackles of fear and uncover the joy and fulfillment that come from authentic connections.

So, let us embark on this transformative journey together, breaking down the barriers that hold us back and embracing the beauty of soulful connections.

Cultivating Self-Compassion

Self-compassion, simply put, is the ability to treat oneself with kindness, understanding, and acceptance, especially in times of struggle or vulnerability. It is about recognizing our own humanity and extending the same understanding and nurture to ourselves that we would offer to a loved one in distress. In essence, it is the foundation upon which genuine and meaningful relationships are built.

In today's fast-paced and demanding world, we often find ourselves caught up in the relentless pursuit of personal and professional success. We become so preoccupied with meeting the expectations of others that we neglect our own emotional well-being and neglect to extend the same empathy and compassion towards ourselves that we eagerly show to others. This lack of self-compassion not only affects our relationship with ourselves but also reverberates through our interactions with others.

When we fail to cultivate self-compassion, we are more likely to judge ourselves harshly, berating ourselves for our perceived shortcomings and failures. This self-judgment creates an internal dialogue that is riddled with negativity and self-doubt, making it difficult for us to truly connect with others on a deep and authentic level. How can we offer genuine empathy and understanding to others when we cannot even extend those same qualities to ourselves?

Research has shown that individuals who practice self-compassion experience improved overall well-being and mental health. They are more resilient in the face of adversity and are better equipped to manage stress. Furthermore, self-compassionate individuals tend to display greater empathy and understanding towards others, as they have learned to cultivate compassion from within. By nurturing a kind and accepting relationship with ourselves, we foster empathy towards others, allowing for a more genuine connection and a deepening of our relationships.

So how can we begin to cultivate self-compassion and foster empathy towards others? It starts with a conscious shift in our mindset and a commitment to tending to our own emotional needs. As we become aware of our own self-judgment and criticism, we can learn to replace these negative thoughts with self-compassionate ones. Instead of berating ourselves for our mistakes, we can choose to acknowledge our humanity and offer ourselves words of kindness and understanding.

Practicing self-care and engaging in activities that bring us joy and nourishment is another important aspect of cultivating self-compassion. Taking time for ourselves, whether it be through hobbies, mindfulness practices, or seeking support from loved ones, allows us to recharge and replenish our emotional reserves. By prioritizing our own well-being, we create a solid foundation from which we can extend empathy and understanding to others.

In conclusion, cultivating self-compassion is not only essential for our own well-being but also for the development of deep and genuine relationships with others. It is through self-compassion that we learn to embrace our own vulnerabilities and extend the same understanding and acceptance to those around us. By nurturing self-compassion within ourselves, we create a ripple effect of empathy and compassion that has the potential to transform our relationships and our world.

Authentic Communication

In our journey towards building genuine relationships, one of the key pillars is authentic communication. But what exactly does it mean to communicate authentically? As a Christian Priest and Counselor with years of experience working with individuals in various stages of life, I have come to understand that authentic communication involves expressing ourselves honestly and sincerely, while genuinely listening and understanding the perspective of others.

In today's fast-paced and technology-driven world, it is easy to fall into the trap of superficial communication.

We often find ourselves hiding behind screens, emojis, or carefully crafted words, afraid to reveal our true thoughts and feelings. However, authentic communication requires us to break down these barriers and create spaces where honesty, vulnerability, and empathy can flourish.

To truly understand the importance of authentic communication, let us consider the context in which it thrives. Authentic communication is not limited to one-on-one conversations; it extends to all aspects of our lives, including our interactions with family, friends, colleagues, and even strangers. It is about fostering connections that go beyond the surface level, allowing us to truly see one another and form meaningful relationships.

Providing practical tips and techniques for effective and authentic communication that nurtures genuine connections:

1. Be present: In a world filled with distractions, being fully present during a conversation is a rare gift. When engaging in authentic communication, make a conscious effort to give your undivided attention to the person you are conversing with. Put away your phone, maintain eye contact, and actively listen without interrupting. By showing that you value their presence, you create a safe space for open and honest communication to flourish.

2. Practice active listening: Authentic communication involves more than just speaking; it requires active listening. When someone shares their thoughts or emotions with you, truly hear them. Avoid the temptation to jump in with your own thoughts or judgments. Instead, focus on understanding their perspective, validating their feelings, and offering support where needed. By actively listening, you convey empathy and create an environment where trust can thrive.

3. Cultivate vulnerability: Authentic communication requires us to embrace vulnerability. This means being open and honest about our own thoughts, feelings, and experiences. By sharing our own stories and struggles, we invite others to do the same, creating a deeper level of connection and understanding. Remember, vulnerability is not a sign of weakness but a strength that allows others to see our authentic selves.

4. Practice empathy and compassion: Authentic communication is rooted in empathy and compassion. Seek to understand the emotions and experiences of others without judgment or agenda. Put yourself in their shoes and genuinely validate their feelings. By showing empathy and compassion, we create an atmosphere of trust and acceptance, nurturing genuine connections.

5. Choose words wisely: Words have the power to heal or harm, so it is crucial to choose them wisely. Practice honest and constructive communication, avoiding harsh or hurtful language. Be mindful of your tone and body language, ensuring that your words align with your intentions. By communicating in a respectful and thoughtful manner, you create an environment where authentic connections can flourish.

As we incorporate these practical tips and techniques into our daily interactions, the art of authentic communication becomes ingrained in our relationships. It is through these genuine connections that we cultivate lasting friendships, foster a sense of belonging, and transform our lives for the better.

Remember, authentic communication is a continuous journey. It requires practice, patience, and a willingness to be vulnerable. But as we embrace this art, we discover the true power of connection and the joy that comes from genuine relationships.

CHAPTER II

The Art of Active Listening

The Essence of Active Listening

Active listening is not merely hearing what someone has to say; it is a conscious and intentional effort to truly understand and empathize with the speaker. It involves giving our undivided attention, not only to the words being spoken but also to the underlying emotions, body language, and subtext. Active listening requires us to be fully present in the moment and engage in a genuine exchange of thoughts and feelings.

One of the fundamental aspects of active listening is the genuine desire to understand the other person. It goes beyond surface-level interactions and seeks to uncover the deeper meanings and motivations behind their words. By actively listening, we create an atmosphere of trust and safety that encourages the speaker to express themselves openly and honestly.

To engage in active listening, we must suspend our own judgments and preconceived notions. Instead of formulating our response while the other person is speaking, we should focus on truly understanding their perspective. This requires patience and practice, as it can be challenging to set aside our own biases and opinions.

The role of active listening in fostering understanding and connection cannot be understated. It is through active listening that we are able to grasp the true essence of what the other person is trying to convey. By being fully present and attentive, we validate their thoughts and emotions, making them feel heard and valued.

Active listening also allows us to build deeper connections with others. When we actively listen, we are able to pick up on subtle cues and hints that may not be expressed explicitly. It is in these nuances that we find opportunities for empathy and compassion, bridging the gap between our own experiences and those of the speaker.

Moreover, active listening helps to cultivate a mutual respect and appreciation for one another. When we give our undivided attention to someone, it conveys a sense of importance and worthiness. This act of validation fosters a sense of belonging and strengthens the bond between individuals.

In my experience working with school and college students, as well as people going through various crises, I have witnessed the profound impact of active listening on their lives. It has been a powerful tool for healing, growth, and self-discovery. By creating a space for individuals to share their thoughts and feelings without judgment, active listening empowers them to find their own solutions and gain a deeper understanding of themselves.

In conclusion, active listening is at the core of building soulful connections. It requires us to be fully present, suspend judgment, and genuinely seek to understand the other person. Through active listening, we foster understanding, empathy, and connection, giving birth to genuine relationships that stand the test of time. As we embark on our journey towards building these soulful connections, embracing active listening will undoubtedly be our guiding light.

Developing Empathetic Listening Skills

Definition and Context:

Empathetic listening is a crucial skill that allows us to truly understand and connect with others on a deeper level. It goes beyond the mere act of hearing and actively engages with the emotions, thoughts, and experiences of the person speaking. As a Christian priest and counselor with years of experience working with students and individuals in crisis, I have witnessed firsthand the transformative power of empathetic listening in building genuine relationships.

In today's fast-paced world, where distractions abound, genuine communication often takes a backseat. We find ourselves constantly preoccupied with our own thoughts and concerns, frequently missing the opportunity to truly engage with others. This lack of empathetic listening not only hampers our relationships but also inhibits the healing and growth that comes from understanding and connecting with others.

Providing practical exercises and techniques to develop empathetic listening skills and enhance communication:

In this chapter, I aim to equip you with practical exercises and techniques that will help you develop and enhance your empathetic listening skills, allowing you to forge deeper, more meaningful connections with those around you.

1. Mindful Listening:

someone is speaking, we are formulating our response in our minds or preoccupied with our own thoughts. Mindful listening requires us to fully focus our attention on the speaker, actively quieting our thoughts and distractions. Through this practice, we create a space where the speaker feels heard and understood.

To cultivate mindful listening, I recommend engaging in daily meditation or mindfulness exercises. These practices help us become more present in the moment, allowing us to shift our attention from our own concerns to the person speaking. Start by setting aside a few minutes each day to sit quietly and observe your thoughts and sensations without judgment. Over time, this practice will enable you to develop a greater level of presence and attentiveness when engaging in conversations.

2. Non-Verbal Communication:

Another essential aspect of empathetic listening is non-verbal communication. Our body language, facial expressions, and gestures play a significant role in conveying empathy and understanding. To enhance your non-verbal communication skills, I encourage you to pay attention to both your own body language and that of the speaker.

Maintain an open and relaxed posture, lean slightly towards the speaker to demonstrate interest, maintain eye contact without staring intently, nod affirmatively to show understanding, and offer appropriate facial expressions that convey empathy and concern. By aligning your non-verbal cues with your intentions to listen empathetically, you create a safe and supportive environment for open and honest communication.

3. Reflective Listening:

To truly understand and connect with others, we need to go beyond simply hearing their words. Reflective listening involves actively reflecting back the speaker's feelings, thoughts, and experiences to demonstrate understanding and empathy. This technique not only validates the speaker's emotions but also fosters a deeper level of trust and connection.

To practice reflective listening, paraphrase what the speaker has said, using your own words, and reflect back the emotions and experiences they have shared. For example, if someone is expressing frustration with a difficult situation at work, you might respond by saying, "It sounds like you're feeling overwhelmed and underappreciated in your current role." This simple act of reflecting their feelings and experiences shows that you are actively listening and trying to understand their perspective.

4. Cultivating Empathy:

Empathy is the cornerstone of any genuine connection. It allows us to step into the shoes of others, understand their experiences, and provide support and understanding. Cultivating empathy involves developing a genuine curiosity and interest in others, suspending judgment, and being open to different perspectives.

To cultivate empathy, I encourage you to engage in empathy-building exercises such as reading books or watching movies that explore diverse perspectives and experiences. Additionally, actively seek out opportunities to engage with individuals from different backgrounds and cultures, as this can broaden your understanding and compassion. With practice, empathy becomes a natural response, enabling you to create deeper and more meaningful connections with those around you.

Conclusion:

Developing empathetic listening skills is an ongoing journey that requires intention and practice. By incorporating mindful listening, non-verbal communication, reflective listening, and cultivating empathy into our daily interactions, we can enhance our ability to genuinely connect with others. As Christians, it is our duty to reach out and support one another, and developing empathetic listening skills is an essential part of fulfilling this obligation. With dedication and perseverance, we can create soulful connections that enrich our lives and the lives of those around us.

Non-Verbal Communication

As a Christian priest and counselor, I have had the privilege of working with diverse groups of people, from school and college students navigating their formative years to individuals grappling with crises in their lives. Throughout my years of experience, one thing has become abundantly clear to me: effective communication extends far beyond the spoken word. In fact, as I delved into the intricacies of human interaction, I discovered that non-verbal cues play a pivotal role in understanding others' emotions and building genuine relationships.

In this chapter, we will delve deep into the realm of non-verbal communication, exploring the power it holds in our daily interactions. I invite you to join me on this journey of unraveling the intricacies of body language, facial expressions, and other non-verbal cues that enable us to truly listen and connect with others on an emotional level.

Step 1: The Art of Observation

To fully grasp the significance of non-verbal cues, we must first cultivate the art of observation. Many of us are so consumed by our own thoughts and perceptions that we fail to notice the intricate details woven into the fabric of every conversation. Becoming an astute observer requires us to be fully present in the moment, attuned to the subtle shifts in body language, and receptive to the unspoken messages conveyed through facial expressions.

Step 2: Decoding Body Language

Body language, often referred to as the "silent language," speaks volumes about a person's emotions and intentions. A simple gesture, a change in posture, or a particular movement of the hands can reveal more than a thousand words. By understanding the nuances of body language, we can gain a deeper insight into someone's feelings, thoughts, and unspoken desires.

Step 3: The Power of Facial Expressions

Our faces are windows to our souls. Countless studies have shown that facial expressions are universally understood, transcending language and cultural barriers. From a genuine smile that radiates warmth to a furrowed brow that indicates concern, our facial expressions provide a direct pathway into our emotions. Mastering the ability to interpret these subtleties allows us to forge connections that go beyond mere words.

Step 4: Emotional contagion and Empathy

As human beings, we are naturally attuned to each other's emotions. The phenomenon of emotional contagion, where emotions are unconsciously transferred from one person to another, is an inherent part of our psychological makeup. By honing our empathy skills, we can not only better understand others' emotions but also provide the support and comfort they need in times of distress. Non-verbal cues serve as guides in this process, signaling the hidden emotions waiting to be acknowledged.

Step 5: Creating a Safe and Nurturing Atmosphere

To encourage open and genuine communication, it is vital to create a safe and nurturing atmosphere where individuals feel comfortable expressing their thoughts and emotions. Non-verbal cues can play a pivotal role in establishing this environment of trust and understanding. From maintaining eye contact to displaying open body language, we can create spaces where others feel seen, heard, and valued.

Step 6: Practicing Mindful Listening

Lastly, effective listening is at the core of building soulful connections. Mindful listening involves not only hearing the words being spoken but also being attuned to the underlying emotions and unspoken messages. By combining our skills in decoding non-verbal cues with active listening, we can deepen our understanding of others' experiences and foster genuine connections that transcend superficial conversation.

Conclusion

In our journey toward building genuine relationships, non-verbal communication acts as the invisible thread that weaves together the tapestry of understanding and connection. By embracing the power of observation, decoding body language and facial expressions, nurturing empathy, and creating safe spaces, we can become adept at forging soulful connections built on a foundation of genuine understanding. Through the art of non-verbal communication, we can truly listen and touch the lives of others in the most profound way possible.

Overcoming Barriers to Listening

In our fast-paced and technology-driven world, it is so easy to get caught up in the distractions that hinder us from truly listening. We may be physically present, but our minds wander and our attention wavers. This lack of focus can create barriers between ourselves and others, preventing us from building the genuine relationships our souls yearn for.

To truly connect with others, we must first identify the common barriers that hinder active listening. One such barrier is our preoccupation with our own thoughts and emotions. We are often so consumed by our own internal dialogue that we fail to fully engage with the person standing before us. We need to recognize when we are lost in our own world and make a conscious effort to shift our focus outward.

Another barrier to listening is our tendency to interrupt or speak over others. We often feel the need to share our own opinions or experiences, disregarding the value of the other person's words. This habit stems from a self-centeredness that prevents us from truly hearing and understanding what the other person is saying. Overcoming this barrier requires humility and a genuine desire to learn from others.

Additionally, distractions in our environment can hinder our ability to listen attentively. The constant buzz of notifications on our phones, the noise of a bustling coffee shop, or even our own physical discomfort can divert our attention away from the person in front of us. To overcome this barrier, we must create an environment of focus and minimize external interruptions, whether it means stepping away from technology or finding a quiet space.

Lastly, emotional barriers can inhibit active listening.

When we harbor negative emotions such as anger or resentment towards someone, our ability to truly listen diminishes. We may become defensive, shutting down any possibility of understanding or empathy. Overcoming this barrier requires self-reflection and a willingness to let go of our emotional baggage, allowing us to approach conversations with a more open and receptive mindset.

Now that we have identified these barriers, the question remains: how do we overcome them? One strategy is to practice mindfulness. By cultivating a present-moment awareness, we can bring ourselves back into the conversation and fully engage with the person speaking. This requires letting go of distractions and focusing our attention on the here and now.

Another strategy is to cultivate empathy. By putting ourselves in the other person's shoes, we can better understand their perspective and truly listen to their words. This means setting aside our own judgments and biases and approaching conversations with a genuine desire to learn and connect.

Lastly, it is important to create space for silence. Sometimes, the most profound connections are made in moments of shared silence. By allowing pauses in the conversation, we can give ourselves and the other person time to process and reflect, resulting in a deeper level of understanding and connection.

Overcoming the barriers to active listening is not a one-time accomplishment, but rather an ongoing practice. It requires a conscious effort to be fully present, to let go of distractions, and to approach conversations with an open heart and mind. As we master the art of genuine listening, we will discover the profound impact it has on our relationships, allowing us to build soulful connections that nourish and enrich our lives.

The Art of Reflective Listening

Reflective listening goes beyond the mere act of hearing words; it involves a heartfelt commitment to truly understand the emotions, values, and experiences being shared by another person. It requires setting aside one's own agenda and ego, focusing solely on the speaker, and creating a safe and non-judgmental space. This art form of listening is indeed an art, one that requires patience, compassion, and empathy.

To embark on the journey of reflective listening, one must start by acknowledging their own assumptions, biases, and preconceived notions. It requires a humble mindset, recognizing that we do not possess all the answers and that the speaker's experience is unique and valid. By suspending judgment, we open ourselves up to hearing the true essence of the other person's story.

As I reflect upon my encounters with individuals in crisis, I am reminded of a young college student named Jaya who reached out to me seeking guidance during a difficult time in her life. Through reflective listening, I was able to create a safe space for her to share her innermost fears and anxieties. With each word she uttered, I listened intently, not only to the content of her words but also to the underlying emotions and values that resonated within her.

Reflective listening involves active engagement, not just passive receptiveness. It requires mirroring back the speaker's thoughts and feelings, ensuring that they feel heard and understood. A gentle nod, a timely pause, or a verbal affirmation can convey our genuine interest in truly comprehending their perspective. In Jaya's case, as she spoke of her struggles with self-doubt and fear of failure, I mirrored back her emotions, saying, "It sounds like you're feeling overwhelmed and uncertain about your future."

Through such reflections, I noticed a profound shift in the depths of our connection. Jaya felt validated and affirmed, knowing that she was truly being heard and understood. As our conversation progressed, she became more comfortable in expressing her vulnerabilities and sharing her dreams and aspirations. Our connection deepened, transcending the roles of priest and counselor to genuine companionship on the journey of self-discovery.

Reflective listening not only nurtures the speaker but also cultivates personal growth within the listener. By honing this art, I have learned to embrace the beauty and diversity of human experiences. Through truly listening, I have discovered how every conversation becomes an opportunity for mutual learning and growth.

In the realm of reflective listening, genuine curiosity plays a pivotal role. By asking open-ended questions and demonstrating a sincere interest in the speaker's perspective, we invite them to delve deeper into their thoughts and feelings. This curiosity helps uncover the layers of meaning and significance behind their words, fostering mutual understanding and fostering a deeper connection.

As I continue to witness the power of reflective listening in building soulful connections, I am reminded of the words of American author Stephen Covey, who once said, "Most people do not listen with the intent to understand; they listen with the intent to reply." In our fast-paced and often self-centered world, the art of reflective listening is a transformative practice that can foster genuine relationships and bridge the gaps that divide us.

In the chapters to come, I will delve further into the intricacies and nuances of reflective listening. I will explore practical techniques and share personal stories that highlight its effectiveness in various contexts. Through these pages, I invite you to join me on this journey of cultivating soulful connections, one genuine conversation at a time. Together, let us embrace the transformative power of reflective listening and unlock the true potential of our relationships.

CHAPTER III

Building Trust and Emotional Intimacy

The Importance of Trust

Examining the significance of trust in relationships, we find that trust encompasses deep emotions such as confidence, reliability, and loyalty. It is the belief that one can rely on another person, confide in them, and have faith in their intentions and actions. Trust is not built overnight; rather, it is cultivated over time through a series of consistent interactions and experiences.

In today's fast-paced and complex world, trust can sometimes feel like a rare gem, hard to find and even harder to keep. We are bombarded with messages of skepticism and distrust, leading us to approach relationships as though they are transactional rather than soulful connections. But the truth is, without trust, relationships lack depth and authenticity.

So how do we build and maintain trust in our relationships? It starts with self-reflection. We must examine our own trustworthiness and evaluate whether our words align with our actions. Are we dependable and consistent in our behavior? Do we show integrity and honesty in our interactions? Building trust is a reciprocal process, requiring both parties to be trustworthy.

Additionally, communication plays a vital role in nurturing trust. Clear and open communication fosters understanding and transparency, enabling individuals to feel secure in expressing their thoughts, concerns, and needs. Active listening, empathy, and validation are crucial components of effective communication, demonstrating respect and fostering trust within a relationship.

Trust can also be strengthened through shared experiences and mutual vulnerability. When we allow ourselves to be vulnerable, opening up about our fears, dreams, and insecurities, we invite others to do the same. This sharing of our authentic selves creates a bond based on trust and empathy, paving the way for deeper connections and fostering an environment of emotional safety.

However, trust, once broken, is not easily repaired. Healing the wounds caused by broken trust requires time, effort, and willingness from both parties to rebuild the shattered foundation. It entails open communication, sincere apologies, and a commitment to change. While forgiveness is essential, it is equally important to establish boundaries and hold each other accountable to prevent further damage.

In conclusion, trust is an invaluable asset in any relationship. It is the thread that binds souls together, allowing for authentic connections to thrive. In our pursuit of genuine relationships, we must recognize the significance of trust and be intentional in its cultivation. By embodying trustworthiness, fostering open communication, and embracing vulnerability, we can build and maintain trust, transforming our relationships into soulful connections that stand the test of time.

Vulnerability and Trust

As I sit down to write about vulnerability and trust, I am reminded of the countless conversations I have had with individuals struggling to build genuine connections in their lives. Over the years, as a dedicated Christian priest and counselor, I have worked with numerous school and college students, as well as those going through various crises. Through these experiences, I have come to understand the immense importance of vulnerability and trust in fostering emotional intimacy.

When we think of vulnerability, we often associate it with weakness or fragility. However, I have come to see vulnerability as the gateway to authenticity and genuine connection. It is the willingness to expose our true selves, flaws and all, to another person, with the hope that they will reciprocate and do the same. It requires courage, for it means risking rejection and judgment. Yet, without vulnerability, we are merely wearing masks, projecting an image of who we think we should be, instead of embracing who we truly are.

Trust, on the other hand, is the solid foundation upon which vulnerability can flourish. It is the belief in the reliability, truthfulness, and integrity of another person. Building trust takes time and effort, as it requires consistency, honesty, and open communication. It means keeping our promises and demonstrating that we can be relied upon. Trust is not easily earned, but when it is established, it creates a safe space for vulnerability to thrive.

The interplay between vulnerability and trust is a delicate dance. It is through vulnerability that we invite trust into our lives, and it is through trust that we find the courage to be vulnerable. This reciprocal relationship creates a bond that allows for emotional intimacy to emerge. Emotional intimacy goes beyond mere physical closeness or shared experiences; it is a deep connection that encompasses mutual understanding, empathy, and unconditional acceptance.

In my work with individuals on their journey towards building genuine relationships, I have witnessed the transformative power of vulnerability and trust. In one particular case, a college student named Ananya came to me feeling isolated and disconnected from her peers. She had always been guarded, afraid to reveal her true thoughts or emotions. Together, we explored the concept of vulnerability, and I encouraged her to take small steps towards openness in her interactions. With time, Ananya began to trust in the support and understanding of others, and gradually she allowed herself to be more vulnerable. Through this process, she discovered a newfound sense of belonging and found herself surrounded by friends who truly understood and accepted her.

It is important to note that vulnerability and trust are not one-time achievements, but ongoing practices. They require constant nurturing and dedication. It is through vulnerability and trust that we peel away the layers of protection we have built around ourselves, allowing others to see our authentic selves. It is a courageous act that invites others to do the same, fostering deeper connections and creating a sense of emotional closeness that is unparalleled.

In conclusion, vulnerability and trust are the cornerstones of building genuine relationships and cultivating emotional intimacy. It is through vulnerability that we reveal our true selves, and it is through trust that we create a safe space for authenticity to flourish. When vulnerability and trust intertwine, they pave the way for emotional intimacy, enabling us to form deep connections with others. Remember, it is in the moments of vulnerability that we truly find ourselves and discover the beauty of soulful connections.

Nurturing Emotional Intimacy

As I reflect on my years of experience as a Christian Priest and Counselor, I am continually reminded of the importance of emotional intimacy in building genuine relationships. Just as the roots of a tree deeply intertwine, so too must our souls connect on a profound level in order to experience true intimacy. In this chapter, I offer practical advice on fostering emotional intimacy and creating a safe space for vulnerability.

To begin, let us acknowledge that emotional intimacy does not develop overnight. It requires time, effort, and a genuine desire to understand and connect with another person deeply. This process demands open communication, active listening, and a willingness to share our own vulnerabilities. By doing so, we create an atmosphere of trust and safety that cultivates the growth of emotional intimacy.

In my work with individuals going through crisis, I have found that one of the most effective ways to nurture emotional intimacy is through active listening. Genuine listening goes beyond hearing the words being spoken; it involves truly understanding the emotions and experiences being shared. By giving our full attention and showing empathy, we validate the feelings of the other person, making them feel heard and understood. This act of validation creates a safe space for vulnerability, where genuine connection thrives.

Furthermore, offering nonjudgmental support is essential in nurturing emotional intimacy. We must set aside our own biases, preconceived notions, and personal agendas, and instead approach the other person with an open heart and mind. By doing so, we create an environment where individuals feel safe to express their fears, insecurities, and deepest desires. Our ability to offer unconditional acceptance allows emotional intimacy to blossom.

In my experiences working with school and college students, I have witnessed the power of creating a safe space for vulnerability through shared experiences. When we allow ourselves to be open and vulnerable, we invite others to do the same. By sharing our struggles, triumphs, and personal growth, we break down the barriers that often hinder emotional intimacy. This act of transparency not only fosters a genuine connection but also inspires others to embrace their own vulnerability.

In building emotional intimacy, we must also recognize the importance of being present in the moment. In our fast-paced, technology-driven world, it is easy to be distracted and disconnected. However, by setting aside our devices, giving our undivided attention, and truly being present with another person, we create a space where emotional intimacy can thrive. This requires active engagement, genuine curiosity, and a willingness to be fully present in the joys and pains of another.

To create a safe space for vulnerability is to create a sanctuary for one's soul. It is a space where individuals can express their emotions, fears, and dreams without fear of judgment or rejection. As a Christian Priest and Counselor, it is my duty to guide individuals in their journey towards emotional intimacy, offering them the tools and support necessary to create these sacred spaces.

In conclusion, nurturing emotional intimacy requires time, active listening, nonjudgmental support, shared experiences, and being fully present. By incorporating these practices into our relationships, we create an environment where vulnerability is embraced, deep connection is forged, and genuine, soulful connections are nurtured. It is my heartfelt hope that by embodying these principles and fostering emotional intimacy, we can cultivate a world filled with authentic relationships and profound understanding.

Rebuilding Trust After Betrayal

As I sit down to write about rebuilding trust after betrayal, I am reminded of the countless individuals I have counseled over the years. Their stories, their pain, and their longing for healing have left indelible imprints on my soul. In my role as a Christian Priest and Counselor, I have witnessed the devastating effects of betrayal and the incredible resilience of the human spirit in the face of such adversity. Trust, once shattered, can feel impossible to reclaim, but with guidance and a steadfast commitment to healing, it is indeed possible.

Step 1: Acknowledge the pain

The journey of rebuilding trust begins with acknowledging the pain caused by betrayal. It is essential to allow yourself to fully experience the depth of your emotions, whether it be anger, sadness, or confusion. This initial step may seem overwhelming, but it is crucial to confront and process these emotions in order to move forward.

Step 2: Identify the root cause

In order to rebuild trust, it is important to understand the root cause of the betrayal. Was it a breach of loyalty, a broken promise, or a violation of boundaries? Identifying the underlying issues will pave the way for addressing them head-on and finding solutions that promote healing and restoration.

Step 3: Seek support

Navigating the path to healing after betrayal can be arduous and at times, lonely. It is essential to seek support from a trusted confidant, be it a close friend, family member, or professional counselor. Exploring your emotions and experiences with someone who can provide guidance and encouragement can be immensely helpful in rebuilding trust and finding solace amidst the pain.

Step 4: Set boundaries

Rebuilding trust requires establishing clear boundaries to protect yourself and regain a sense of safety. Boundaries help define acceptable behavior and expectations, creating a framework in which trust can flourish. Communicating these boundaries to those who have betrayed you allows for open dialogue and an opportunity to establish a new foundation built on mutual respect.

Step 5: Practice forgiveness

Forgiveness is a pivotal aspect of rebuilding trust after betrayal. However, forgiveness does not mean forgetting or condoning the actions that caused the betrayal. Instead, it is a conscious choice to release the pain and resentment that may be holding you captive. Forgiveness allows you to reclaim your own power and move forward towards healing.

Step 6: Rebuilding trust through consistent actions

Trust is rebuilt through consistent actions over time. These actions must align with words, demonstrating a genuine commitment to change and growth. Trust is a fragile entity, and it requires patience and understanding as you navigate the uncertainty of rebuilding what was lost. By consistently showing integrity and accountability, those who have betrayed you can begin to restore the trust that was broken.

Step 7: Cultivate self-compassion

Throughout the process of rebuilding trust, it is crucial to cultivate self-compassion. Self-blame and self-judgment can hinder your ability to heal and move forward. Remember, betrayal is a reflection of the betrayer's actions, not of your worth or value as a person. Embrace self-care practices, engage in activities that bring you joy, and surround yourself with a supportive community that reinforces your resilience.

In conclusion, the journey of rebuilding trust after betrayal requires courage, patience, and a commitment to healing. It is a process that demands self-reflection, open communication, and forgiveness. Trust, once shattered, can be pieced back together through consistent actions, genuine remorse, and a shared commitment to growth. As you embark on this transformative journey, do not underestimate the strength within you to rebuild and establish even stronger and more soulful connections.

Trust-Building Exercises

In my journey of guiding others in cultivating trust, I have found that providing interactive exercises and activities can be instrumental in strengthening trust and fostering emotional connection. These exercises aim to create a comfortable, safe space for individuals to open up, share vulnerabilities, and build a foundation of trust. Here, I will share with you some of the effective trust-building exercises and activities that I have used successfully.

One of the exercises that I have found particularly impactful is the "Two Truths and a Lie" game. This activity encourages individuals to share three statements about themselves, two of which are true and one that is false. The rest of the group then engages in a lively discussion, trying to identify the lie. This exercise not only helps in breaking the ice but also encourages participants to share personal anecdotes, creating a sense of vulnerability and authenticity. Moreover, as the group members share their opinions and debate which statement is true or false, it fosters an atmosphere of active listening and respectful communication, further reinforcing trust within the group.

Another exercise that has proven effective in building trust is the "Trust Walk." In this activity, participants pair up and one person is blindfolded while the other acts as their guide. The guide then leads the blindfolded person through a predetermined route, relying solely on verbal instructions and trust in their partner. The blindfolded person must surrender control, placing complete faith and trust in their guide. This exercise not only encourages individuals to rely on one another but also promotes effective communication, active listening, and the capacity to let go of control. Through this vulnerability and reliance on each other, participants are able to build a deeper level of trust.

Additionally, a powerful trust-building exercise is the "Circle of Appreciation." In this activity, participants sit in a circle, and each person takes turns expressing their appreciation for another individual in the group. The expressions of appreciation may range from acknowledging someone's strengths or positive qualities to expressing gratitude for their support and friendship. This exercise creates an atmosphere of positivity and validation, allowing individuals to feel seen, acknowledged, and valued by others. By openly showing appreciation for one another, participants develop a sense of trust and emotional connection within the group.

These exercises and activities are just a few examples of the countless opportunities available to build trust in relationships. The key lies in providing a safe and nurturing environment where individuals can develop the confidence to be vulnerable and authentic. It is through this authenticity and vulnerability that trust flourishes, enabling individuals to form deep, soulful connections.

As I continue to guide and counsel individuals, I have realized that trust-building exercises are not one-time solutions but ongoing practices that require consistent effort and intentionality. By embracing these exercises and incorporating them into our daily lives, we can foster trust, emotional connection, and ultimately build genuinely fulfilling relationships.

CHAPTER IV

Boundaries and Self-Care

The Role of Boundaries in Relationships

They are essential for fostering a sense of self and autonomy within a relationship, while also acknowledging and respecting the other person's individuality. Without boundaries, we risk crossing the fine line between genuine connection and codependency.

One of the first steps in setting boundaries is understanding and articulating our own needs and values. This self-awareness allows us to clearly communicate our expectations and limits to others. Open and honest communication is crucial in any relationship, as it enables both parties to understand each other's boundaries and work together to establish common ground. By expressing our needs and asserting our limits, we allow both ourselves and the other person to know where we stand, creating a foundation of respect and understanding.

Establishing boundaries also requires a willingness to enforce them with assertiveness and consistency. Many individuals struggle with setting boundaries because they fear confrontation or the possibility of disappointing others. However, it is important to remember that setting boundaries is an act of self-care and self-respect. When we allow others to violate our boundaries without consequence, we compromise our sense of self and open the door to resentment and frustration.

Boundaries also protect us from toxic and unhealthy relationships. They act as a filter, allowing only those who are willing to respect and honor our boundaries to remain in our lives. By saying no to behaviors that are unacceptable or compromise our well-being, we create space for healthier relationships to flourish. Boundaries serve as a clear signal to others about our standards and expectations. Those who understand and honor these boundaries are more likely to form genuine connections with us built on respect and mutual understanding.

Finally, it is important to remember that boundaries are not rigid and inflexible. They can and should be revisited and revised as our needs change and grow. As we evolve and adapt, our boundaries may shift accordingly. This flexibility enables us to continuously nurture and maintain healthy relationships based on open and honest communication.

In conclusion, the setting of boundaries plays a vital role in building and sustaining healthy and respectful relationships. By understanding and articulating our own needs and values, enforcing them consistently with assertiveness, and evaluating and adapting our boundaries when necessary, we create an environment where genuine connections can thrive. Boundaries act as the compass that guides us towards fulfilling and satisfying relationships, allowing us to navigate the path towards soulful connections.

Communicating Boundaries Effectively

Introduction:

As humans, we all desire and deserve healthy relationships, where mutual respect and understanding flourish. However, to create these soulful connections, we must learn the art of communicating boundaries effectively. Boundaries serve a vital role in protecting our mental, emotional, and physical well-being. They are the invisible lines that define our limits, needs, and expectations in any given relationship. In this chapter, I will provide practical tips and strategies for communicating boundaries in a clear and compassionate manner, fostering deeper connections and personal growth.

Step 1: Self-awareness and Understanding Boundaries

Before we can effectively communicate our boundaries to others, we must first be aware of our own needs, limits, and values. This requires introspection, reflection, and a keen understanding of our emotional landscape. Identifying what is acceptable and respectful behavior for ourselves allows us to establish healthy boundaries. Take the time to explore your values, needs, and triggers. Consider what makes you feel uncomfortable or violated in relationships. Reflect on past experiences to cultivate a deeper self-awareness, as this will be the foundation upon which you communicate your boundaries effectively.

Step 2: Be Clear and Direct in Your Communication

Once you have identified your boundaries, it is crucial to communicate them clearly and directly to those around you. Avoid giving mixed messages or assuming that others will automatically understand what you need. Clearly state your limits, expectations, and consequences if those boundaries are crossed. Remember, the goal is not to control or manipulate others, but rather to assert yourself and ensure your well-being. Speak assertively yet respectfully, using "I" statements to express your feelings and needs. For example, instead of saying, "You always make me feel guilty," say, "I feel guilty when this happens."

Step 3: Practice Active Listening

Effective communication involves both expressing yourself and actively listening to others. When someone else shares their boundaries, truly listen and take their needs into account. Seek to understand their perspective and validate their emotions. Active listening fosters empathy and respect, creating a safe space for open dialogue. Reflect back what you have heard to ensure you have understood correctly and to demonstrate your genuine interest in the other person's well-being. By actively listening, you cultivate a culture of mutual respect and understanding within your relationships.

Step 4: Boundaries and Consequences

It is essential to establish consequences for boundary violations as a means of reinforcing their importance and protecting your well-being. Communicate these consequences clearly and stick to them if necessary. By setting and enforcing these boundaries, you empower yourself and demonstrate self-respect, while also teaching others how to treat you. However, it is important to differentiate between healthy consequences and punishment. Healthy consequences should be logical, fair, and aimed at restoring respect and balance in the relationship, rather than seeking revenge or control.

Step 5: Seek Support and Professional Help

Communicating boundaries effectively can be challenging, especially in complex or deeply ingrained relationships. Seek support from trusted friends, family, or mentors who can provide guidance and validation. Additionally, consider reaching out to a professional counselor or therapist who can offer insights and techniques specific to your situation. They can help navigate the intricacies of setting boundaries and provide a safe space to explore and address any underlying issues that may be hindering your ability to communicate effectively.

Conclusion:

Mastering the art of communicating boundaries requires self-awareness, clear and direct communication, active listening, consequences, and seeking support when needed. These practices will empower you to foster healthy, respectful relationships and promote your overall well-being. Remember, establishing boundaries is not about building walls, but rather creating a foundation of trust, understanding, and intimacy. By effectively communicating boundaries, we lay the groundwork for soulful connections that nurture and uplift all parties involved. So take these practical tips and strategies and embark on a journey of building genuine relationships founded on mutual respect and acceptance.

Self-Care as a Foundation

Self-care goes beyond simply pampering ourselves with occasional massages or indulging in our favorite hobbies. It is a holistic approach to nurturing our physical, mental, and emotional well-being. It entails paying attention to our needs, setting healthy boundaries, and cultivating habits that promote self-love and self-respect.

Research has consistently shown that individuals who practice self-care are more likely to have better mental health, higher self-esteem, and stronger relationships.

When we take the time to recharge and replenish our own energy, we are better equipped to be present for others and engage in deep and meaningful connections.

In my counseling sessions with students and individuals going through crisis, I often emphasize the importance of self-care as a foundation for building healthy relationships. It is not uncommon for people to neglect their own needs while trying to be everything to everyone else. However, this approach is unsustainable and eventually leads to burnout and resentment.

Self-care is an act of self-love that allows us to restore balance and take care of our own needs. When we prioritize our well-being, we become more attuned to our own feelings, desires, and boundaries. We are better able to communicate our needs effectively and establish healthy boundaries in our relationships.

Moreover, practicing self-care teaches us the invaluable lesson of self-respect. When we prioritize our own well-being, we send a message to ourselves and others that we are worthy of love and care. This radiates through our interactions with others and attracts like-minded individuals who value and appreciate us for who we are.

In Soulful Connections, I guide readers to explore various self-care practices that can be incorporated into their daily lives. From mindfulness exercises and journaling to developing healthy eating habits and engaging in regular exercise, the possibilities for self-care are endless. I provide practical tips and techniques for integrating self-care into even the busiest of schedules, emphasizing that self-care is not a luxury but a necessity.

By highlighting the importance of self-care, I hope to encourage readers to prioritize their own well-being and recognize that their personal happiness and fulfillment are vital to building genuine relationships. When we make self-care a foundation in our lives, we create a solid base from which to nurture and sustain meaningful connections with others. It is through caring for ourselves that we can show up fully for others, not just as mere acquaintances or surface-level connections, but as soulful individuals capable of fostering deep and authentic relationships.

Respecting Others' Boundaries

First and foremost, it is vital to recognize that everyone has different boundaries, shaped by their unique life experiences and personal values. What may seem like a harmless comment or action to one person can be deeply intrusive or offensive to another. The key lies in cultivating empathy and actively listening to those around us. By doing so, we can gain a deeper understanding of the boundaries that exist within each individual, and adjust our behavior accordingly.

To truly respect the boundaries of others, we must also be willing to communicate openly and honestly. This involves not only expressing our own boundaries but also actively seeking feedback from others. Too often, we assume that others have the same boundaries as us, leading to potentially harmful misunderstandings. By engaging in open dialogue, we can bridge the gap between our intentions and the impact we have on others, ultimately strengthening our connections.

In our quest to respect the boundaries of others, it is important to acknowledge our own limitations. As humans, we are fallible, and there may be times when we inadvertently overstep someone's boundaries. In such instances, it is crucial to take responsibility for our actions, offering sincere apologies and seeking ways to rectify the situation. By demonstrating humility and a willingness to learn from our mistakes, we can rebuild trust and reaffirm our commitment to respecting the boundaries of others.

Additionally, technology and social media have drastically altered the landscape of human interaction, often blurring the lines that define personal boundaries. It is essential to recognize the significance of consent and privacy in the digital age. Online platforms provide us with unprecedented access to personal information, and it is imperative that we handle this access with sensitivity and respect. Seeking explicit consent before sharing someone's personal details or engaging in online discussions about sensitive topics can go a long way in preserving trust and fostering healthy connections.

Respecting the boundaries of others is not merely an act of etiquette or politeness; it is a fundamental expression of love and care. When we consciously strive to understand and honor the boundaries of those around us, we create an environment where individuals feel safe to be their authentic selves. In fostering this culture of respect, we lay the foundation for soulful connections that are grounded in trust, acceptance, and genuine empathy.

As we navigate the intricacies of building genuine relationships, let us remember that respecting the boundaries of others is not a one-time task; it is a lifelong commitment. In each interaction we have, may we approach others with an open heart and mind, valuing their individuality and cherishing the unique boundaries they bring to the table. Together, let us embark on a journey that embodies the art of building soulful connections, one boundary at a time.

Balancing Boundaries and Flexibility

As I sit here, pen in hand, contemplating the essence of genuine relationships, I cannot help but delve into the topic of balancing boundaries and flexibility. It is a delicate dance, a fine art that requires both tact and intuition. In my years as a Christian priest and counselor, I have had the privilege of working closely with individuals from all walks of life, including school and college students, as well as those navigating through life's crises. Through these encounters, I have come to understand that finding the sweet spot between setting firm boundaries and being adaptable is crucial for mutual growth and understanding.

Setting boundaries is an essential aspect of any relationship, be it with a partner, a friend, or a colleague. Boundaries help define the limits of what is acceptable, ensuring that our needs and values are respected. They serve as an invisible line, safeguarding our well-being and integrity. However, there is a fine line between setting healthy boundaries and becoming rigid, unyielding in our expectations. Too often, we mistakenly believe that the act of setting boundaries implies a defensive stance, an unwillingness to compromise. Yet, in my experience, I have found that when boundaries are set with love and empathy, they foster trust and create a safe space for deeper connections to flourish.

To strike this balance, one must first be aware of their own needs and limitations. It requires self-reflection and introspection – a willingness to identify what truly matters to us and what we are willing to compromise on. This self-awareness enables us to communicate our boundaries effectively, allowing the other person to understand our limits and values. However, it is important to remember that boundaries should never be imposed forcefully; instead, they must be presented with humility and respect. By doing so, we honor both ourselves and the other person, acknowledging that our individuality is an intrinsic part of any authentic relationship.

Flexibility, on the other hand, acts as the catalyst for growth and understanding in relationships. It is the ability to adapt and adjust, to navigate the ebbs and flows that life presents. Flexibility embraces change and embraces the idea that no relationship is static. Relationships, like life itself, are constantly evolving, and our capacity to be flexible contributes to their longevity. Being flexible entails being open-minded, willing to listen and learn from one another. It means recognizing that compromise is not a sign of weakness but rather a testament to the strength of the relationship itself.

A relationship that finds the delicate balance between boundaries and flexibility is one in which both parties feel seen, heard, and understood. It is a harmonious dance, where each partner acknowledges and respects the other's boundaries, while also being willing to adapt and grow together. It is important to remember that finding this balance is an ongoing journey – one that requires patience, empathy, and constant communication.

As I reflect on the multitude of relationships I have witnessed and nurtured over the years, I am reminded of the innate beauty in the art of balancing boundaries and flexibility. It is a testament to the human spirit – that we are individuals with unique needs, desires, and dreams, yet we also yearn for connection, support, and love. It is through this delicate dance that we uncover the true essence of soulful connections – the art of building genuine relationships.

CHAPTER V

Cultivating Empathy and Compassion

Understanding Empathy and Compassion

In our journey towards building genuine connections, it is essential that we delve into the depths of empathy and compassion. These two concepts are like gentle bridges that traverse the vast chasm of human emotions and experiences, enabling us to truly understand and connect with one another. As a Christian priest and counselor who has dedicated numerous years to working with individuals in crisis, as well as school and college students, I have witnessed the transformative power of empathy and compassion firsthand. Allow me to take you on an exploration of these concepts and their role in fostering soulful connections.

Empathy, at its core, is the ability to step into someone else's shoes, to experience their joys, sorrows, and struggles as if they were our own. It is like a light that illuminates the path of understanding and acceptance, enabling us to connect with others on a deeper level. When we practice empathy, we open our hearts and minds to the experiences of others, allowing their stories to resonate within us.

To truly empathize, we must be willing to set aside judgment and preconceived notions. We must be humble enough to acknowledge that we may never fully comprehend another person's experiences, but we can listen with an open heart, seeking to understand their perspective. Empathy requires both active listening and genuine curiosity. It calls us to be fully present, to offer our undivided attention to the person before us, and to validate their feelings and emotions.

Compassion, on the other hand, is the natural response that arises when empathy takes root within us. It is the heartfelt desire to alleviate the suffering of others and to act in ways that promote their well-being. Compassion is a wellspring of love, kindness, and generosity that flows from the depths of our souls. It calls us to extend a helping hand, to offer words of encouragement, and to provide support and solace to those in need.

When we approach others with empathy and compassion, we create a sacred space where vulnerability is embraced, and healing can occur. These tools of connection enable us to build bridges rather than walls, to foster genuine relationships rather than superficial acquaintanceships. They empower us to reach beyond our own experiences and to connect with the universal human experience.

Research has shown that practicing empathy and compassion not only benefits others but also enhances our own well-being. Studies have indicated that individuals who exhibit higher levels of empathy and compassion experience reduced levels of stress, increased feelings of fulfillment, and improved overall mental health. Empathy and compassion not only nurture the souls of those who receive them but also enrich the souls of those who give them.

So, my dear friends, let us embark on this journey of understanding empathy and compassion. Let us open our hearts to the experiences of others, listening with a genuine desire to comprehend their realities. Let us cultivate compassion within ourselves, extending love and kindness to all those we encounter. Together, we can build a world rooted in soulful connections, where empathy and compassion are valued and nurtured.

Developing Empathy Skills

As human beings, one of the most powerful tools we possess for building genuine relationships is empathy. It enables us to step outside our own perspectives and truly connect with others by understanding their experiences and emotions. In this chapter, I will provide practical exercises and techniques to cultivate empathy and comprehend others' perspectives, transforming the way we relate to one another.

Exercise 1: Practicing Active Listening

Empathy can only be truly developed when we actively listen to others. It is not merely about hearing their words; it is about creating a safe space for them to express themselves fully. To practice active listening, choose a partner and engage in a conversation where you take turns speaking and listening. While your partner speaks, focus your attention on their words, body language, and tone of voice. Avoid interrupting or formulating your response while they speak. Instead, aim to genuinely understand their thoughts and emotions before expressing your own.

Exercise 2: Stepping into Someone Else's Shoes

One way to enhance empathy is by consciously putting ourselves in someone else's shoes. This exercise requires imagination and openness. Choose a person in your life whose perspective you find challenging to understand. For a moment, imagine yourself stepping into their shoes, seeing the world through their eyes, and feeling what they might feel. Reflect on their experiences, background, and the challenges they may have faced. This exercise allows you to broaden your perspective and develop compassion for others' unique journeys.

Exercise 3: Practicing Self-reflection

Empathy not only involves understanding others but also understanding ourselves. By engaging in self-reflection, we develop a deeper awareness of our own biases, beliefs, and experiences that shape our interactions with others. Take moments of solitude to reflect on your own emotions, values, and beliefs. In doing so, you will gain insight into your own motivations and reactions, allowing you to approach relationships with a greater sense of empathy and understanding.

Technique 1: Empathetic Body Language

Non-verbal communication plays a crucial role in cultivating empathy. Our body language conveys messages that speak louder than words. By consciously adopting empathetic body language, we can create an environment of trust and connection. Maintain eye contact, position yourself at an open angle, nod and smile to indicate your attentiveness and engagement. These small gestures signal to others that you are present and genuinely interested in what they have to say.

Technique 2: Asking Open-ended Questions

To foster empathy in our relationships, it is essential to encourage open and honest dialogue. Asking open-ended questions allows others to share their thoughts and feelings more freely. Avoid questions that can be answered with a simple yes or no. Instead, ask questions that encourage deeper introspection and invite others to express themselves fully. This technique promotes a sense of trust, as people feel heard and valued when given the opportunity to share their experiences openly.

Research has shown that empathy is not only beneficial for building relationships but also for personal growth and well-being. It strengthens our emotional intelligence, increases our compassion, and enhances our problem-solving abilities. By cultivating empathy, we create a world where understanding, compassion, and genuine connections flourish.

In conclusion, developing empathy skills requires both practice and self-reflection. Through active listening, stepping into someone else's shoes, and engaging in self-reflection, we can expand our capacity for empathy. By adopting empathetic body language and asking open-ended questions, we create an environment that fosters meaningful connections. Let us embark on this journey together, building soulful connections through the art of empathy.

Compassionate Communication

In my many years as a Christian priest and counselor, I have come to realize that communication lies at the heart of every relationship. It is through our words and actions that we connect with others, and it is through effective and compassionate communication that we build genuine and meaningful relationships.

But what exactly is compassionate communication, and why is it so important in fostering understanding within relationships? Allow me to guide you through the depths of this topic, as we explore how we can communicate with compassion and create stronger connections with those around us.

At its core, compassionate communication is the art of speaking from the heart and listening with empathy. It involves expressing ourselves honestly and authentically, all while being sensitive to the feelings and needs of others. This type of communication is centered around love and understanding, and it requires us to cultivate qualities such as patience, kindness, and emotional intelligence.

In today's fast-paced and technological world, it is easy to fall into the trap of quick and shallow communication. We find ourselves sending texts or emails rather than engaging in face-to-face conversations. However, genuine relationships require depth and connection, which can only be achieved through compassionate communication.

To begin our journey towards compassionate communication, we must first understand the context in which it is most needed. Relationships, whether they be with our partners, friends, family members, or colleagues, often encounter challenges. Miscommunication, misunderstandings, and conflicts are inevitable in any human interaction. However, it is how we choose to navigate these challenges that determines the strength and longevity of our relationships.

Throughout my work with school and college students, as well as individuals going through crisis, I have witnessed firsthand the power of compassionate communication in resolving conflicts and healing wounds. When we approach difficult conversations with an open heart and a willingness to understand, rather than attack or defend, we create a safe space for both ourselves and others to express our thoughts and feelings. In this safe space, the weight of judgment and hostility dissipates, leaving room for empathy and compassion to flourish. It is in these moments, where we suspend our own biases and preconceptions, that true connection and understanding can bloom.

As we navigate challenging conversations, it is essential to remind ourselves of the power of listening. Listening not only to the words spoken but also to the emotions and intentions behind them. It is in this act of attentive listening that we can truly comprehend the nuances of someone else's perspective. We refrain from assuming, interrupting, or formulating counterarguments prematurely. Instead, we allow their words to settle in our minds, digesting them fully before crafting a thoughtful response.

Patience becomes our ally as we resist the urge to rush the conversation. We recognize that meaningful dialogue takes time and effort. Like tending a delicate garden, we must cultivate an environment where thoughts and ideas can thrive, unperturbed by the hurried pace of life. In doing so, we foster an atmosphere where trust and respect can take root, enabling a deeper exploration of the intricacies surrounding the topic at hand.

Understanding, however, does not always equate to agreement. It is crucial to acknowledge that everyone possesses their own unique set of experiences, beliefs, and values. We respect these differences and recognize that the diversity of perspectives enriches our understanding of the world. By embracing this vast tapestry of thoughts, we challenge our own biases and expand our horizons. Through respectful exchange, we may find common ground or realize that differing viewpoints can coexist harmoniously.

Amidst these challenging conversations, it is paramount to remain mindful of the impact of our words. We aim to communicate with intention, ensuring that our message is delivered in a manner that is firm yet gentle, assertive yet considerate. We avoid inflammatory language or personal attacks, understanding that such approaches only serve to entrench divisions further. Instead, we choose to reintroduce civility into discourse, recognizing the transformative power that respect and kindness hold.

True growth and progress emerge from conversations where all parties feel heard and validated. When we approach difficult dialogues with patience, empathy, and an unwavering commitment to understanding, the barriers that divide us begin to crumble. Each conversation becomes a stepping stone towards a more united, compassionate, and enlightened world.

So let us embark on this journey of discourse with open hearts and inquisitive minds, ready to listen, learn, and bridge the gaps that divide us. For it is through these courageous conversations that we realize our shared humanity and manifest the potential for a brighter future.

Empathy in Conflict Resolution

Conflict, a ubiquitous reality in human life, arises from a multitude of sources - differing opinions, contrasting values, and unmet needs. It has the potential to tear relationships apart, leaving a trail of hurt and bitterness in its wake. However, when wielded with intention and grace, empathy can turn the tide of conflict, paving the way for genuine connections and profound healing.

As a counselor and priest, I have had the privilege of witnessing the transformative power of empathy in the resolution of countless conflicts. Whether working with school and college students struggling with peer pressure, or individuals navigating the storms of a personal crisis, I have seen first-hand how empathy can break down barriers and restore harmony.

In order to truly understand the depth and impact of empathy in conflict resolution, we must first delve into its essence. At its core, empathy is far more than mere sympathy or compassion. It requires a profound connection to the emotions, thoughts, and experiences of another person, allowing us to walk in their shoes and see the world through their eyes. It is an act of vulnerability, opening ourselves up to the rawness of another's pain, and offering them solace and understanding.

To embark on the journey of empathy in conflict resolution, we must recognize and acknowledge the context in which we find ourselves. Every conflict has its unique set of circumstances, histories, and emotions. By placing ourselves in the center of this intricate web, we can begin to unravel the intricacies of the conflict, and ultimately, foster an environment of mutual understanding and growth.

Empathy in conflict resolution also requires us to engage with our own emotions and biases. It is far too easy to approach conflicts with preconceived notions or a desire to be right. However, true empathy calls for the suspension of judgment, allowing us to truly listen and absorb the perspectives of others. It compels us to challenge our own assumptions and beliefs, fostering an environment conducive to compassion and transformation.

Furthermore, empathy is not a passive act; it requires action and commitment. In conflict resolution, empathy compels us to actively seek out opportunities for dialogue, to engage in open and honest conversations that lay the foundation for reconciliation. It pushes us to embrace discomfort and vulnerability, knowing that the path to resolution is often paved with difficult conversations and challenging emotions.

Through empathy, conflicts can become not battlegrounds for power and ego, but rather fertile ground for mutual growth and healing. It allows us to view conflicts as opportunities for connection, fostering relationships that are stronger, deeper, and more resilient. Empathy invites us to transcend the constraints of our individual perspectives, and in doing so, encourages shared understanding and compassion.

In soulful connections, empathy takes center stage as the guiding force towards genuine relationships. It empowers us to navigate the complexities of conflicts, transforming them into catalysts for personal and collective growth. By embracing empathy in conflict resolution, we can pave the way for a world where understanding and compassion prevail, and where genuine connections thrive.

Spreading Compassion Beyond Relationships

In the ever-evolving world we live in, it is imperative that we foster compassion beyond the boundaries of our personal connections. In this section, my sincere aspiration is to inspire readers to embrace and cultivate a spirit of compassion that extends far beyond their immediate circle.

Compassion, often regarded as a fundamental quality of humanity, has the power to transform not only our individual lives but also the very fabric of society. It is a force that propels us towards understanding, empathy, and positive action. However, in our fast-paced lives and often self-focused tendencies, we often overlook the profound impact that compassion can have on our own well-being, as well as the well-being of those around us.

To truly cultivate a spirit of compassion that transcends personal connections, we must first acknowledge the innate interconnectedness of all beings. Recognizing that each person we encounter is on their own journey, facing their own struggles and triumphs, allows us to develop a sense of empathy that extends beyond our immediate acquaintances. This realization becomes the foundation on which our compassion can flourish.

Furthermore, it is essential to develop a sense of curiosity and openness towards others and their experiences. By broadening our perspective beyond our usual social circles, we can gain profound insights into the diverse realities that exist beyond our immediate sphere of influence. Engaging in meaningful conversations, either face-to-face or through various mediums, enables us to bridge the gap of understanding and foster a sense of compassion that is inclusive and expansive.

In addition, compassion extends beyond mere sentiment; it demands action. True compassion requires us to go beyond feeling empathetic and actually take steps to alleviate the suffering of others. Whether it be volunteering our time, donating resources, or advocating for impactful change, our actions can make a significant difference in the lives of those in need. It is through these acts of compassion that we cultivate a profound sense of fulfillment and purpose.

As we journey through this section, it is my hope that readers will not only gain a deeper understanding of the importance of cultivating compassion but also be inspired to implement it in their daily lives. By extending our compassion beyond our personal connections, we have the power to create a ripple effect of positive change in the world.

Let us embark on this transformative journey together, as we aspire to transcend our own limitations and embrace a spirit of compassion that knows no boundaries.. I strongly believe that each one of us has the power to make a difference in the lives of others, regardless of our circumstances or the scope of our influence. By tapping into our innate capacity for empathy, we can spread compassion far and wide, infusing it into every aspect of our lives and the lives of those we touch.

Compassion is often thought of as an emotion, a feeling of deep sympathy and concern for the suffering of others. While this is undoubtedly true, it is also so much more. Compassion is a verb; it is an action that requires dedication, intention, and practice. It involves actively seeking ways to alleviate the suffering around us, to understand and empathize with the struggles of others, and to extend a helping hand when needed.

But how can we spread compassion beyond our personal relationships? How can we make a positive impact in the world, even if our sphere of influence may appear limited? The answer lies in recognizing the interconnectedness of all beings and understanding that small acts of kindness can have ripple effects that reach far and wide.

First and foremost, it is important to cultivate self-compassion. We must learn to treat ourselves with the same kindness and understanding that we extend to others. By nurturing a deep sense of self-love, we set a strong foundation upon which we can build genuine connections and spread compassion. Self-compassion allows us to approach relationships with a genuine desire to understand and support others, rather than seeking validation or personal gain.

Next, we must broaden our horizons and open our minds to the suffering of those beyond our immediate circles. This requires stepping outside of our comfort zones and seeking opportunities to engage with individuals from different backgrounds, cultures, and communities. By expanding our perspectives, we gain a deeper understanding of the diverse challenges faced by people across the globe. This, in turn, fuels our compassion and fuels our desire to make a difference.

One powerful way to spread compassion is through acts of service. Whether it be volunteering at a local charity, contributing to a cause close to your heart, or simply lending a helping hand to a neighbor in need, each act of service has the potential to not only transform the lives of those directly impacted but also to inspire others to do the same. By leading by example, we become beacons of light in a world that craves compassion and solidarity.

Moreover, spreading compassion beyond relationships requires us to use our voice and share stories of hope and resilience. Through writing, speaking, or advocating for specific causes, we can raise awareness of the issues affecting others and inspire action. Our words have the power to spark empathy, challenge societal norms, and motivate those around us to make a positive impact.

Lastly, we must recognize the importance of self-reflection and introspection in spreading compassion beyond relationships. By regularly examining our intentions, behaviors, and attitudes, we can ensure that our actions are aligned with our values and contribute to the greater good. It is through this inner work that we refine our character, deepen our empathy, and become more effective vessels for spreading compassion in the world.

In conclusion, spreading compassion beyond relationships is both a noble calling and a profound responsibility. It is a lifelong journey of self-discovery, growth, and selfless action. By extending our empathy and compassion to those beyond our personal connections, we can help create a world that is more united, more just, and more compassionate. Let us embark on this journey together, hand in hand, as we strive to build a better world, one act of kindness at a time.

CHAPTER VI

Navigating Differences and Conflict

Embracing Diversity in Relationships

As I reflect upon my years of experience as a Christian priest and counselor, working with individuals from diverse backgrounds, it becomes increasingly clear to me that embracing diversity is a crucial aspect of building genuine and meaningful relationships. In a world marked by many differences - be it race, ethnicity, religion, culture, or even personal interests and preferences - it is essential that we learn to appreciate and celebrate the unique qualities that each person brings to a relationship.

Diversity, in its essence, is a treasure trove of opportunities for growth and understanding. It invites us to step outside of our comfort zones, expand our horizons, and encounter perspectives that may challenge our own. When we open ourselves to the richness of diversity, we gain a deeper understanding of the world and its inhabitants, fostering a stronger sense of compassion and empathy towards one another.

However, embracing diversity does not imply merely tolerating differences or turning a blind eye to the disparities that exist. It requires a genuine commitment to inclusivity, acceptance, and respect for every individual, regardless of their background or beliefs. It is about creating a safe space where everyone's voice is heard and validated.

In order to celebrate the beauty of diversity, we must first acknowledge our own biases and prejudices. Each one of us possesses unconscious biases, shaped by our upbringing, education, and societal norms. These biases have the potential to hinder our ability to truly embrace and appreciate the differences that others bring. Recognizing and addressing these biases is the first step towards cultivating inclusivity in our relationships.

Moreover, we must actively seek opportunities to learn from others. Engaging in conversations with individuals who hold differing viewpoints, beliefs, or experiences can broaden our own understanding of the world. Listening attentively and respectfully to their stories and perspectives not only enriches our knowledge but also provides us with new lenses through which we can view the world.

While celebrating diversity means appreciating our differences, it also involves finding common ground with others. In the midst of our diversity, we are bound by our shared humanity, and it is important to find those threads that connect us. By focusing on our shared values, aspirations, and experiences, we can forge genuine connections that transcend cultural or societal barriers.

Building relationships that embrace diversity requires patience and a willingness to navigate through uncertainties and misunderstandings. It may involve discomfort and the need to confront difficult conversations. However, it is through these challenges that we grow individually and collectively.

In this chapter, I aim to provide guidance on embracing differences in relationships, illustrating the beauty and value that diversity brings. Through personal anecdotes and vignettes from my counseling experience, I share stories of individuals who have successfully navigated the complexities of diversity, illuminating the profound impact it can have on our relationships.

Ultimately, embracing diversity in relationships is a testament to our recognition of the inherent worth and dignity of every person. It is a celebration of the vibrant tapestry of humanity and a commitment to building a more inclusive and compassionate world. Together, let us embark on this journey of embracing diversity, for it is in the embrace of our differences that we truly discover the richness of our shared humanity.

Communicating Through Conflict

In this section, I would like to offer practical tips and techniques for effective communication during times of conflict and disagreement. I firmly believe that by approaching conflicts with empathy, understanding, and a genuine desire for resolution, we can transform these challenging situations into opportunities for growth and deeper connection.

Step 1: Seek Understanding

The first step in communicating through conflict is to seek understanding. Often, conflicts arise from miscommunication or misunderstandings. Take the time to really listen to the other person's perspective and try to put yourself in their shoes. Ask open-ended questions to encourage them to share their feelings and views. By seeking to understand their point of view, you can create an atmosphere of empathy and respect, laying the foundation for constructive dialogue.

Step 2: Express Yourself Clearly

While seeking to understand the other person's perspective, it is equally important to express your own thoughts and feelings clearly and assertively. Use "I" statements to express how the conflict has impacted you personally, avoiding blame or judgment. Clearly articulate your needs and expectations, without attacking the other person's character or integrity. Remember, effective communication is not about winning an argument but finding a resolution that meets both parties' needs.

Step 3: Practice Active Listening

Active listening is a crucial skill in resolving conflicts. Show that you are fully present and attentive by maintaining eye contact, nodding your head to indicate understanding, and providing verbal cues such as "I see," or "I understand." Avoid interrupting or formulating your response while the other person is speaking. Instead, truly listen to their words, emotions, and body language. By actively engaging in the conversation, you demonstrate respect for the other person's perspective and increase the likelihood of finding common ground.

Step 4: Manage Emotions

Conflicts can evoke strong emotions, making it challenging to communicate effectively. It is essential to manage your own emotions during these moments, as well as acknowledge and validate the emotions of the other person. Take a deep breath, count to ten, or even take a short break if necessary. By taking the time to regulate your emotions, you can approach the conflict with a calmer mindset and prevent escalating tensions. Additionally, showing empathy towards the emotions of the other person can help to de-escalate the conflict and create a safe space for open dialogue.

Step 5: Collaborate towards a Solution

The ultimate goal in communicating through conflict is to find a resolution that satisfies both parties. Collaborative problem-solving involves brainstorming ideas, exploring alternative perspectives, and working together to find a compromise or win-win solution. This requires a willingness to look beyond individual differences and focus on mutual understanding and respect. Be open to new ideas and be willing to let go of rigid positions in order to find common ground.

By following these steps, we can navigate through conflict with grace and integrity, fostering genuine relationships built on trust and understanding. It is my hope that these practical tips and techniques will empower you to communicate effectively, even during the most challenging moments of disagreement. Remember, conflicts do not have to divide us; they can be opportunities to deepen our connections and grow as individuals and communities.

Active Problem-Solving

To guide my readers in mastering the art of active problem-solving, I have developed a step-by-step guide that I have found to be effective in my own counseling work. These steps not only promote a healthy approach but also encompass the spiritual and emotional aspects of the process. By integrating these elements, individuals can tackle even the most challenging of problems with grace and perseverance.

Step 1: Define the Problem

The first step in any problem-solving process is to clearly define the problem at hand. Often, individuals are overwhelmed by the multitude of issues they face and struggle to identify the core problem. To overcome this, I encourage readers to take a step back and reflect on their situation. Through introspection, one can gain a deeper understanding of the issue and its root causes. Defining the problem is like identifying the target: without a clear target, we cannot hit the bull's-eye.

Step 2: Seek Support and Guidance

Once the problem is defined, the next crucial step is to seek support and guidance. Humans are social creatures, and no problem is insurmountable when faced together. Whether it be a trusted friend, a family member, or even a professional counselor, finding someone to lend an empathetic ear and provide objective advice can make a world of difference. In my counseling sessions, I have seen firsthand the transformative power of opening up and seeking the wisdom of others. It takes humility and vulnerability but embracing these qualities will lead to a deeper connection and a better chance at finding a win-win solution.

Step 3: Explore Alternatives

In active problem-solving, exploring a variety of alternatives is instrumental. Often, individuals get stuck in a cycle of repetitive thinking, unable to see beyond the immediate limitations. By encouraging readers to step outside their comfort zones and consider different possibilities, they can break free from constraints and discover innovative solutions. This process requires creativity and an open mind, as well as the willingness to take risks. It involves considering not only the present circumstances but also the long-term consequences, both for oneself and others involved. By exploring alternatives, readers can broaden their perspective and unlock new opportunities that were previously unseen.

Step 4: Collaborative Communication

Communication is the cornerstone of any relationship, and when it comes to active problem-solving, it becomes even more critical. Throughout my career, I have witnessed the damaging effects of poor communication in relationships, hindering the resolution of conflicts and perpetuating misunderstandings. To avoid such pitfalls, I guide readers to adopt a collaborative communication approach. This involves active listening, expressing oneself clearly and honestly, and ensuring that all parties involved have an equal voice in the conversation. By fostering an atmosphere of mutual understanding and respect, individuals can collectively work towards finding win-win solutions.

Step 5: Evaluate and Implement

The final step in active problem-solving is to evaluate and implement the chosen solution. It is necessary to assess the feasibility and effectiveness of the proposed solution against the defined problem. I urge readers to consider the potential outcomes, both immediate and long-term, and ensure that they align with their values and principles. This step also requires perseverance, as setbacks and challenges are inevitable once the solution is implemented. By remaining steadfast and committed, individuals can navigate through obstacles and experience true growth.

By following these steps, readers will be equipped with the tools needed to approach problem-solving collaboratively and find win-win solutions. Active problem-solving is not merely a transactional process but rather a transformative journey that builds genuine relationships with oneself and others. I have witnessed the beauty of active problem-solving in my counseling work, and I am confident that by embracing this approach, readers can unlock their potential to create soulful connections and lead fulfilling lives.

The Power of Forgiveness

Forgiveness is not just a one-time act, but rather an ongoing process of letting go and choosing to extend compassion and understanding to those who have hurt us. It requires us to set aside our ego and our desire for vengeance, and instead, seek reconciliation and restoration. Through forgiveness, we create a space for healing, growth, and the nurturing of genuine connections.

When I think about forgiveness, I am reminded of a verse from the Bible, Matthew 18:21-22, where Jesus teaches the importance of forgiving not just seven times, but seventy-seven times. This teaching emphasizes the limitless nature of forgiveness and the need to continually extend grace and mercy to those who have wronged us. It is a powerful reminder that forgiveness is not a one-time event but a practice that we must cultivate daily.

Research has shown that forgiveness not only benefits the individual who extends it but also has a positive impact on their relationships. A study conducted by the University of Miami found that forgiveness leads to greater marital satisfaction and decreased psychological distress in couples. Through forgiveness, couples are able to rebuild trust, communicate more effectively, and navigate through conflict with grace and understanding.

Furthermore, forgiveness has been proven to have significant health benefits. A study published in the Journal of Behavioral Medicine revealed that individuals who practiced forgiveness experienced lower levels of stress, improved immune function, and decreased symptoms of depression and anxiety. The act of forgiveness reduces the toxic emotions associated with holding grudges and promotes emotional and physical well-being.

In my experience as a counselor, I have witnessed the transformative power of forgiveness in the lives of individuals who have chosen to let go of past hurts and embrace forgiveness. I have seen broken marriages mended, friendships restored, and families reconciled through the practice of forgiveness. It is a journey that requires vulnerability, courage, and a willingness to let go of our pain and anger. But in doing so, we create the space for healing, growth, and the building of genuine connections.

To embark on the journey of forgiveness, it is important to recognize that it does not mean condoning or forgetting the actions that have caused us harm. Rather, it is a conscious decision to choose love and compassion over bitterness and resentment. It is an act of self-care that liberates us from the weight of emotional baggage and allows us to move forward in our relationships with a renewed sense of hope and wholeness.

I invite you to reflect upon any unresolved conflicts or hurts in your own life and consider the power of forgiveness as a pathway towards healing and growth. As we learn to let go of past hurts and extend forgiveness to others, we open ourselves up to the profound beauty of genuine connections. Let us embrace the transformative power of forgiveness and forge soulful connections that can withstand the tests of time and adversity.

Building Bridges, Not Walls

In today's world, where discord and division seem to be the norm, it has become imperative for us to take a step back and reconnect with what truly matters – genuine relationships built on understanding and unity. As I reflect upon my experiences as a Christian priest and counselor, working closely with school and college students, as well as those going through personal crises, I am acutely aware of the importance of building bridges, not walls.

To bridge divides and forge connections across differences, it is crucial for us to challenge the barriers that separate us. We must be willing to acknowledge and embrace our differences, rather than allowing them to divide us further. It starts with recognizing that diversity is not a threat, but rather a treasure trove of unique perspectives, experiences, and gifts that can enrich our lives immeasurably.

One of the key aspects of building bridges is fostering deep understanding. We must go beyond surface-level interactions and truly seek to comprehend others' viewpoints and experiences. This requires active listening, empathy, and a genuine interest in stepping into someone else's shoes. When we invest the time and effort to understand others, we not only lay the foundation for truly meaningful connections, but we also dismantle the walls of prejudice and bias that often lurk within us.

True understanding is not just limited to intellectual comprehension; it extends to the realm of the heart. It is through the power of compassion and love that we can foster a sense of unity among diverse individuals. When we genuinely care for one another, we are able to empathize with each other's joys and sorrows, hopes and fears. This empathy forms the basis for building trust and strengthening relationships, even in the face of differences.

In order to inspire readers to bridge divides, it is essential to address the fears and insecurities that often hinder us from reaching out to others. It is through addressing these deep-seated emotions that we can guide individuals towards embracing vulnerability and taking risks to forge connections. By acknowledging the discomfort that arises when we step outside our comfort zones, we can alleviate the fear of the unknown and encourage readers to approach differences with an open mind and heart.

Additionally, it is crucial to provide readers with practical tools and strategies to overcome barriers and create bridges. These may include communication techniques that foster understanding, conflict resolution skills that promote peaceful dialogues, and strategies for cultivating an inclusive mindset. Equipped with these tools, readers can navigate the complexities of relationships with authenticity, grace, and a commitment to building unity.

As I continue to share my insights and experiences in guiding individuals towards building bridges instead of walls, I am reminded of the profound impact this work has on both individuals and communities. Soulful connections born out of genuine understanding and unity have the power to transform lives, heal wounds, and bridge divides that may have seemed insurmountable.

So, dear reader, I implore you to join me on this journey of soulful connections. Let us together dismantle the walls that separate us and instead build bridges that foster understanding, unity, and love. Embrace the diversity that surrounds us, listen deeply to others' stories, and be willing to step outside your comfort zone. Together, we can create a world where bridges stand tall amidst the sea of divisiveness, reminding us of our shared humanity and the beauty that lies in celebrating our differences.

CHAPTER VII

Cultivating Gratitude and Appreciation

The Power of Gratitude

To truly grasp the power of gratitude, we must first explore the science behind it. Numerous studies have shown that gratitude has a direct impact on our mental and emotional health. When we express gratitude, our brain releases dopamine and serotonin, neurotransmitters responsible for feelings of joy and pleasure. This flood of positive chemicals not only uplifts our own spirits but also has a ripple effect on those around us, creating a more positive and conducive environment for meaningful interactions.

Moreover, gratitude has been found to enhance our overall well-being by reducing stress and anxiety. When we cultivate gratitude, we shift our focus from what is lacking in our lives to recognizing and appreciating the abundance that surrounds us. This change in perspective allows us to approach challenges with resilience and optimism, promoting a healthier mindset and improving our ability to navigate through difficult times. By practicing gratitude, we are better equipped to handle conflicts and misunderstandings in our relationships, fostering a deeper sense of understanding and empathy.

Psychology also sheds light on the impact of gratitude in building and strengthening relationships. One of the most remarkable aspects of gratitude is its ability to foster reciprocity. When we express gratitude towards others, we not only acknowledge and appreciate their contributions, but we also create an emotional connection and sense of indebtedness. This motivation to reciprocate kindness and support strengthens the bond between individuals, forming the foundation of genuine relationships built on trust and mutual respect.

Furthermore, gratitude serves as a powerful antidote to the toxic and self-centered dynamics that can plague relationships. By cultivating gratitude, we are less likely to take our loved ones for granted and more inclined to express appreciation for their presence and efforts. This simple act of gratitude can have profound effects, such as boosting self-esteem, enhancing communication, and fostering a deep sense of belonging and connection. When both sides of a relationship actively practice gratitude, a reciprocal cycle of appreciation and support is established, creating a resilient and fulfilling connection.

In summary, the power of gratitude cannot be underestimated when it comes to building genuine relationships and fostering personal well-being. The scientific and psychological research behind gratitude demonstrates its profound impact on our mental and emotional health, as well as its ability to enhance our relationships. By actively cultivating gratitude in our lives, we can create a ripple effect of positivity, strengthen our connections with others, and experience a deep sense of fulfillment and joy. Let us embrace the power of gratitude and unlock its transformative potential in our lives.

Cultivating a Grateful Mindset

In order to cultivate a mindset of gratitude, it is important to provide practical exercises and techniques that individuals can incorporate into their daily lives. These exercises serve as a gentle reminder to intentionally focus on the positives rather than dwelling on the negatives. One such exercise is the practice of gratitude journaling.

Gratitude journaling involves taking a few moments each day to write down three things for which you are grateful. This simple act of reflection allows us to shift our attention away from the challenges and difficulties we may be facing, and instead redirects our focus towards the blessings and joys that we often overlook. By consistently engaging in this practice, we train our minds to actively seek out the positive aspects of our lives, leading to a more optimistic outlook overall.

Another effective technique in cultivating a grateful mindset is the practice of expressing appreciation directly to the people in our lives. This can be done through heartfelt conversations, handwritten notes, or even small gestures of kindness. By verbalizing our gratitude and appreciation, we not only uplift the spirits of those on the receiving end, but we also deepen our own sense of connection and gratitude.

Furthermore, it is essential to acknowledge that cultivating a grateful mindset goes beyond simply focusing on the good things in our lives. It also involves an acceptance and appreciation of the challenges and hardships we face. These difficulties, though painful, often provide us with valuable opportunities for growth and transformation. By reframing our perspective and finding gratitude even in the midst of adversity, we can navigate life's trials with resilience and grace.

Research has shown that individuals who actively cultivate a grateful mindset experience a myriad of benefits in their relationships. They are more empathetic and understanding towards others, as they approach interactions with a sense of gratitude for the opportunity to connect and communicate. This gratitude spills over into relationships, fostering an environment of trust, support, and mutual respect.

In conclusion, cultivating a grateful mindset is not an overnight transformation, but rather a lifelong journey. It requires consistent practice and dedication to consciously shift our focus towards gratitude. By incorporating practical exercises such as gratitude journaling and expressing appreciation, we can actively cultivate a mindset of thankfulness in our daily lives and relationships. As we embrace gratitude, we open ourselves up to a deeper connection with ourselves, others, and the world around us, ultimately leading to soulful and genuine relationships.

Expressing Appreciation

One of the most effective ways to express appreciation is through sincere and specific words of thanks. When we take the time to acknowledge and verbalize our gratitude for the actions, qualities, or presence of another person, it not only affirms their worth but also strengthens the bond between us. Whether it is a simple "thank you" or a more detailed and heartfelt expression, the act of appreciating others allows us to communicate our love, respect, and recognition for who they are and what they contribute to our lives.

However, expressing appreciation should not be limited to words alone. Actions often speak louder than words, and it is important to demonstrate our gratitude through our behavior. This can be as simple as doing a small favor for someone, showing kindness in our interactions, or actively listening and being present when they are speaking. These actions not only communicate our appreciation but also show that we value and care for the other person.

Creating a culture of gratitude within relationships requires consistent effort and intention. It involves fostering an environment where expressing appreciation becomes the norm rather than the exception. One way to do this is by setting an example ourselves. When we make it a habit to express gratitude and appreciation regularly, it encourages others to do the same.

Furthermore, we need to be mindful of the specific ways in which different individuals prefer to receive appreciation. Some people may respond best to verbal affirmations, while others may appreciate acts of service or gifts. Taking the time to understand and cater to the unique preferences of those we are in relationship with shows that we genuinely care about them and value their happiness.

In addition to individual expressions of appreciation, creating a culture of gratitude can also be fostered through collective efforts. This can include implementing gratitude practices within families, workplaces, or communities. For example, establishing a routine of sharing gratitude during meal times or dedicating a regular meeting to express appreciation for team members' efforts can strengthen relationships and create a positive atmosphere.

Research has shown that expressing appreciation has numerous benefits for both the giver and recipient. It has been linked to increased happiness, improved well-being, and strengthened relationships. When we take the time to express our gratitude, we not only uplift others but also experience a profound sense of joy and fulfillment ourselves.

In conclusion, expressing appreciation is a powerful tool that can transform our relationships and create a culture of gratitude. By using sincere and specific words of thanks, demonstrating our gratitude through actions, and fostering an environment where appreciation is valued, we can build strong and authentic connections with others. Let us embrace the art of expressing appreciation and witness the profound impact it has on our relationships and overall well-being.

Gratitude in Challenging Times

It is undeniable that life can be filled with trials and tribulations - moments that test our emotional fortitude and threaten to break our spirit. Whether it is the loss of a loved one, financial struggles, or the burdensome weight of a chronic illness, it is easy to succumb to feelings of despair and hopelessness. However, I firmly believe that in the midst of these challenges, gratitude has the power to transform our perspective and infuse us with renewed strength and resilience.

When we are faced with adversity, it is natural to focus on the negative aspects of our situation. Our minds become consumed with thoughts of all that we have lost or the seemingly insurmountable obstacles in our path. However, gratitude offers a different lens through which to view our circumstances. It shifts our attention towards what remains, the blessings that still surround us, no matter how small or seemingly insignificant they may be.

Research has shown that practicing gratitude can have a profound impact on our mental and emotional well-being. It has been found to reduce levels of stress, anxiety, and depression, while also improving our overall sense of happiness and life satisfaction. But how does gratitude achieve such extraordinary results?

When we choose to intentionally focus on what we are grateful for, it redirects our attention away from our hardships. It allows us to acknowledge the goodness that still exists in our lives, no matter how faint it may be. This shift sparks a subtle transformation within us, cultivating a mindset of abundance rather than scarcity.

Gratitude is not merely a passive acknowledgement of the positive aspects of our lives; it is a deliberate and active choice to seek out and appreciate the blessings that surround us, even in the midst of adversity. It is in this active practice that we find the true power of gratitude – the power to reframe our perspective, to find beauty in the midst of chaos, and to cultivate a sense of hope and resilience that can carry us through even the darkest of times.

In my work as a Christian Priest and Counselor, I have witnessed countless individuals who have embraced gratitude as an integral part of their healing journey. They have learned to find solace in the simplest of blessings – a warm cup of tea in the morning, the comforting embrace of a loved one, or the gentle whisper of the wind in the trees. By consciously directing their attention towards gratitude, they have found the strength to endure and the courage to continue on their path towards healing.

Gratitude in challenging times does not imply that we need to ignore or minimize our pain. It is important to acknowledge our struggles and allow ourselves to grieve. Yet, in the midst of our pain, we can also choose to find pockets of gratitude that act as anchors, grounding us in the present moment and reminding us of the beauty and resilience of the human spirit.

So how can we cultivate gratitude in the face of adversity? It begins with a willingness to shift our perspective and a commitment to actively seek out moments of gratitude. It may be as simple as keeping a gratitude journal, where we record daily blessings and moments of joy. It may involve sharing our gratitude with others, expressing appreciation for their presence and support in our lives. Or it may require engaging in acts of service and kindness, recognizing the immense value of giving and receiving.

In moments of darkness, it is gratitude that shines a light, illuminating the path towards healing and resilience. It is a powerful tool that allows us to reframe our experiences and find strength where we thought there was none. As we navigate life's challenges, let us embrace gratitude as a lifeline, holding on tightly and allowing it to ignite hope and renewal within us.

Gratitude as a Way of Life

As I sit down to write this chapter, my heart feels overwhelmed with gratitude for the opportunity to explore such a profound concept with all of you. Gratitude is not merely a feeling or a passing moment of appreciation, but rather a way of life that has the power to transform our relationships and bring immense joy and fulfillment.

Amidst the chaotic world we find ourselves in, it is easy to overlook the simple blessings that surround us every day. We rush through each moment, constantly seeking the next best thing, forgetting to pause and express gratitude for what we already have. But what if I told you that by incorporating gratitude into our lives, we can elevate our relationships to new heights and cultivate a deep sense of contentment?

In today's society, where comparison and competition dominate our thoughts, it is vital for us to shift our focus towards gratitude. It is through embracing a mindset of appreciation that we can truly recognize and value the beauty in the world around us. When we appreciate the simple things - a warm cup of tea, the sound of laughter, or a kind word from a loved one - we begin to cultivate an attitude of gratitude that spills over into every aspect of our lives.

Research has shown that actively practicing gratitude has immense psychological and emotional benefits. It can reduce stress and anxiety, improve sleep, and even boost our overall well-being. Moreover, grateful individuals tend to have healthier and more fulfilling relationships. By expressing appreciation for our loved ones, we not only make them feel valued and cherished, but we also foster open lines of communication and deepen our connection with them.

Now, you may be wondering how we can cultivate a lifestyle of gratitude amidst the busyness and challenges of everyday life. The answer lies in shifting our perspective and making gratitude a daily practice. One powerful way to do this is by keeping a gratitude journal. Each day, take a few moments to reflect on the blessings that filled your day and jot them down. It could be something as simple as witnessing a beautiful sunset or receiving a kind gesture from a stranger.

In addition to journaling, I encourage you to infuse gratitude into your daily interactions. Whether it's expressing appreciation for a colleague's hard work or simply saying thank you to a loved one, these small acts of gratitude can have a profound impact on our relationships. Moreover, by consciously seeking out opportunities to show gratitude, we become more attuned to the positive aspects of our lives.

Through the practice of gratitude, we not only transform our relationships, but we also transform ourselves. We become more present, more compassionate, and more aware of the beauty and blessings that surround us. Gratitude becomes a lens through which we view the world, and it opens our hearts to the abundance of love and joy that exists within and around us.

So, my dear readers, I invite you to step into this beautiful journey of gratitude. Let us embrace the transformative power of appreciation and make gratitude a way of life. Together, let us create soulful connections that are built on the foundation of gratitude, and watch as love, joy, and fulfillment flow effortlessly into our lives.

CHAPTER VIII

Sustaining Soulful Connections

Cultivating Relationship Rituals

As a seasoned Christian Priest and Counselor, I have come to understand the significance of rituals in building genuine and lasting relationships. Rituals hold a sacred space within our lives, providing a sense of stability, connection, and meaning. They are the threads that weave the fabric of our relationships, anchoring us when we feel lost or disconnected.

In this chapter, we will delve deeper into the importance of rituals in relationships and explore the various ways we can create meaningful and nurturing rituals. These rituals, when practiced with intention and commitment, have the power to strengthen our bonds and bring us closer to our loved ones.

The concept of rituals goes far beyond the religious practices we often associate them with. While religious rituals have their own significance and hold a special place in many people's lives, the focus here is on the rituals we create within our interpersonal connections. These rituals can be as simple as a shared morning coffee routine, a weekly date night, or even a bedtime ritual before retiring for the night.

Research shows that engaging in rituals promotes a sense of belonging and security within a relationship. It creates a shared history, a set of memories that are unique to the couple or individuals involved. These rituals act as markers in time, reminding us of our commitment, love, and dedication to one another.

One idea for a meaningful ritual is to establish a weekly "gratitude night" with your partner or loved one. Set aside a specific evening each week to reflect on the things you appreciate and are grateful for in your relationship. Take turns expressing what you value about one another, your shared experiences, and the ways in which you have grown together. This practice not only fosters a deeper connection but also cultivates an attitude of gratitude and appreciation.

Another ritual that can nurture a relationship is a monthly "adventure day." Choose one day each month to embark on a new and exciting activity together. This could be exploring a new city, trying a new hobby, or even taking a cooking class together. The essence of this ritual is to step out of your comfort zone and experience something new as a couple. It allows for growth, shared excitement, and the creation of memories that will be cherished for years to come.

In addition to these suggestions, it's essential to customize your rituals to suit your unique relationship dynamic and individual preferences. Perhaps you and your partner both enjoy reading; you may establish a nightly ritual of reading a chapter from a book aloud to one another. Or, if you and your loved one are nature enthusiasts, you might create a monthly ritual of hiking to a new trail and enjoying the beauty of the outdoors together.

Remember, the key to cultivating meaningful and nurturing rituals lies in intentionality and consistency. Make a conscious effort to prioritize these rituals in your lives, even when other commitments or distractions arise. Treat them as sacred practices that hold profound significance in your relationship. Rituals have the power to bring you closer, to deepen your connection, and to remind you of the love and commitment you share.

Prioritizing Quality Time

Quality time is not merely about spending time with loved ones; it is about investing in meaningful connections and building lasting memories together. It is about carving out undivided attention for one another, making each moment count, and creating a safe space for vulnerability and emotional intimacy to flourish. In essence, quality time lays the foundation for soulful connections.

So, how do we prioritize quality time and ensure that it becomes an integral part of our relationships? Here are some guiding principles that I believe can transform the way we approach and value this essential aspect of human connection.

First and foremost, we must recognize the importance of making intentional choices. In my years of counseling, I have often encountered individuals who express regret over not having spent enough time with loved ones when they had the chance. Life is unpredictable, and we cannot afford to take our relationships for granted. Therefore, we must be proactive in setting aside dedicated time for our loved ones, making them a priority in our lives.

Setting boundaries is another crucial aspect of prioritizing quality time. In a society that glorifies busyness and multitasking, it is imperative to establish boundaries that protect our relationships. This may involve switching off our devices during meals, designating specific times for family activities, or even saying "no" to certain commitments that may encroach upon our precious moments together. Remember, quality time requires a conscious effort to create an environment free from distractions and interruptions.

Moreover, we should consider engaging in activities that promote authentic connection and shared experiences. Research has shown that engaging in novel and exciting activities together can strengthen emotional bonds and enhance relationship satisfaction. This can involve exploring new hobbies together, planning adventurous outings, or simply taking the time to have meaningful conversations that go beyond the surface level. By actively seeking out opportunities to create lasting memories, we create a solid foundation for genuine and soulful connections.

Additionally, it is crucial to emphasize the need for active listening and open communication during quality time. Too often, we are physically present but mentally absent, preoccupied with our own thoughts or distracted by external factors. True quality time requires active engagement, where we listen attentively, express our thoughts and emotions honestly, and truly connect with one another on a deeper level. By being fully present during our time together, we validate each other's feelings and foster a sense of mutual understanding.

Lastly, but certainly not least, we must learn to be flexible and adaptable in our approach to quality time. Life is unpredictable, and circumstances may not always align with our plans. However, if we are willing to adopt a flexible mindset and seize the opportunities that arise, we can still create meaningful moments amidst the chaos. It could be as simple as stealing a few minutes to have a heartfelt conversation in the midst of a busy day or planning spontaneous date nights to break the monotony. The key is to embrace the spontaneity and beauty that life offers and make the most of every opportunity to build genuine connections.

In conclusion, prioritizing quality time is an art that requires mindful reflection and intentional choices. By recognizing its significance, setting boundaries, engaging in meaningful activities, actively listening, and being adaptable, we can create lasting memories and forge soulful connections. Let us embark on this journey together and make every moment count in our pursuit of genuine and fulfilling relationships.

Continual Growth and Learning

As I delve into the topic of genuine relationships and the art of building them, it becomes evident that personal growth and learning play a vital role in this process. The growth of an individual not only contributes to their own well-being but also creates a strong foundation for nurturing relationships and fostering mutual development.

In my years of experience as a Christian priest and counselor, I have worked with a diverse range of individuals, including school and college students as well as people going through various crises. Through these interactions, I have witnessed firsthand the transformative power of continual growth and learning in strengthening relationships.

Research shows that individuals who prioritize personal growth tend to have a better understanding of themselves and are more self-aware. This self-awareness forms the bedrock upon which healthy relationships can be cultivated. When individuals embark on a journey of self-discovery and growth, they are better equipped to identify and address their own needs, emotions, and limitations.

This, in turn, enables them to enter into relationships with a greater sense of self-assuredness and authenticity.

Furthermore, continuous learning allows individuals to expand their knowledge and perspectives, broadening their understanding of the world and its inhabitants. When we engage in lifelong learning, we open ourselves up to new ideas, cultures, and experiences. This enriched awareness enables us to connect with others on a deeper level, fostering empathy, compassion, and mutual understanding.

In the realm of relationships, the importance of personal growth and learning becomes even more pronounced. Stagnation can be a significant roadblock to building genuine connections, as it hinders our ability to adapt, respond, and grow alongside our loved ones. However, when we are committed to our own growth, it creates an environment of continual development within our relationships.

Consider this: when we are constantly learning and growing, we become more adaptable and open-minded. We are more willing to listen, understand, and accommodate the changing needs of our loved ones. This adaptability not only strengthens our connections but also encourages our partners, friends, or family members to embark on their own journeys of growth and lifelong learning. Through our example, we inspire and motivate those around us to seek personal growth and embrace the transformative power it offers.

In nurturing relationships, continual growth and learning serve as a catalyst for mutual development. When both individuals are actively seeking personal growth, it creates a dynamic environment where learning becomes a shared experience. Together, partners can explore new hobbies, attend workshops or classes, or engage in meaningful conversations that enhance their understanding of each other and the world around them.

Moreover, the willingness to learn and grow together fosters trust and intimacy within relationships. By acknowledging that we are imperfect beings who are continuously evolving, we create a space of acceptance and mutual support. When challenges arise, as they inevitably do, this shared commitment to growth allows us to navigate them hand in hand, strengthening the bond between us.

It is important to remember that personal growth is an ongoing journey. Just as relationships require consistent effort, so too does our own development. Embracing the value of continual growth and learning enables us to approach our relationships with intention, authenticity, and a willingness to adapt and evolve.

By prioritizing personal growth and lifelong learning, we not only enhance our own lives but also create an environment conducive to building and nurturing genuine relationships. Let us remember that growth is not just an individual pursuit but something that thrives within the context of relationships. Together, let us embark on a journey of self-discovery and growth, supporting one another while building soulful connections that transcend time and circumstance.

Navigating Life Transitions Together

Life is full of transitions, both planned and unexpected. From graduating school and starting a new job to getting married and having children, each transition brings with it a shift in our roles, relationships, and responsibilities. These transitions can be exhilarating and joyful, but they can also be challenging and overwhelming. As we journey through these changes, it is essential to have a strong support system in place to navigate the inevitable ups and downs.

In this section, I want to offer guidance on how to navigate life transitions as a team and support each other through change. Based on my years of experience as a Christian priest and counselor, I have witnessed the power of genuine relationships during these transformative periods. Drawing from these experiences and insights, I hope to provide you with practical tools to help you guide and support one another as you navigate the twists and turns of life.

Step 1: Open Communication

During times of transition, communication is key. It is crucial to create a safe and open space where everyone involved can express their fears, hopes, and expectations. This requires honest and transparent conversations, where each person feels heard and understood. As a team, it is essential to listen actively and validate each other's emotions, even if they differ from our own. By practicing empathy and active listening, we foster an environment where everyone feels comfortable sharing their thoughts and concerns.

Step 2: Identify and Acknowledge Change

Before we can navigate a transition, it is vital to identify and acknowledge that change is happening. Often, we resist change, clinging to familiar routines and habits. However, by embracing change and accepting that it is an inevitable part of life, we can begin the process of adapting and growing together. Encourage each other to reflect on how the transition will impact your lives individually and collectively. By recognizing the change, you can better prepare for it and respond to any challenges that may arise.

Step 3: Set Realistic Expectations
Transitions can be accompanied by high expectations and pressures. It is important to recognize that everyone's experience will be unique, and it is unrealistic to have the same expectations for each person. As a team, discuss and set realistic goals that take into account each person's strengths, limitations, and desires. By doing so, you can alleviate unnecessary stress and foster an environment that values individual growth and support.

Step 4: Seek Professional Guidance
Throughout a life transition, seeking professional guidance from counselors, mentors, or clergy can be invaluable. These individuals have the training and experience to provide guidance and support during uncertain times. As a team, consider reaching out to professionals who specialize in the specific transition you are navigating. They can offer insight, strategies, and encouragement to help you navigate the challenges that come with change.

Step 5: Cultivate a Supportive Community
Building a supportive community is paramount in successfully navigating life transitions. Surround yourself with individuals who will cheer you on, celebrate your victories, and offer a shoulder to lean on when things get tough. Lean on each other for support and be intentional in nurturing and maintaining these relationships. Through shared experiences and mutual support, you will find strength, encouragement, and resilience as you journey through life's many transitions.

As you embark on this journey of navigating life transitions together, remember that change can be an opportunity for growth, deeper connections, and self-discovery. Approach these transitions with open hearts and minds, placing value on the relationships and connections that sustain and empower you. Together, you can weather any storm and emerge stronger, wiser, and more interconnected than ever before.

Celebrating and Honoring Connections

As I sit in my study, surrounded by the warmth emanating from a flickering candlelight., I reflect on the countless souls I have encountered throughout my journey as a Christian priest and counselor. Each person, with their unique story and struggles, has taught me the extraordinary power of genuine connections. Here, I invite you to join me on a journey of celebrating and honoring the soulful connections that have shaped and nourished our lives.

Gratitude is a profound emotion that has the ability to transform our perspective, igniting a flame of joy and contentment within our hearts. It is a spiritual practice that fosters deep appreciation for the love and support we have received from those who have touched our lives. When we express gratitude for our connections, we not only acknowledge the impact they have had on us but also strengthen the bonds that hold us together.

Imagine for a moment the joy that fills a room when loved ones gather to celebrate a momentous occasion. The laughter, tears, and heartfelt embraces are a testament to the cherished relationships we have nurtured. In these moments of celebration, gratitude blooms like a radiant sunflower, permeating our being with love and warmth.

In the hustle and bustle of our daily lives, we sometimes forget to pause and express gratitude for the connections that sustain us. We become so consumed by our own ambitions and desires that we overlook the blessings of friendship, family, and community that surround us. However, it is in these relationships that we find solace and strength during challenging times. They provide us with the support we need to navigate life's winding path.

As you turn the pages of this chapter, I encourage you to reflect on the soulful connections you have forged. Think of the kindred spirits who have stood by you through thick and thin, the mentors who have guided you with wisdom, and the dear friends who have brought laughter and light into your life. Each of these connections has played an integral role in shaping the person you are today.

To honor our connections is to recognize the immeasurable value they bring to our lives. It is in this act of honoring that we breathe life into the bonds we cherish. Through simple gestures of appreciation, such as expressing our gratitude through kind words, offering a heartfelt embrace, or even dedicating a moment of prayer, we nourish the connections that sustain us.

In our journey of celebrating and honoring connections, let us remember that oftentimes, it is not the grand gestures that hold the most power, but rather the sincerity and intention behind them. A handwritten note expressing gratitude to a loved one, a small act of kindness, or simply being present for someone in need can create ripples of love and appreciation that extend far beyond what we can imagine.

As I conclude, I invite you to take a few moments to close your eyes and picture the faces of those who have touched your soul. Let their voices echo within your heart, reminding you of the love and support that has carried you through life's trials and tribulations. In this space of gratitude, let us commit ourselves to celebrating and honoring these connections not only today but every day, for they are the threads that weave the tapestry of our lives.

CHAPTER IX

The Magic of Small Gestures

The Language of Love

Chapter 4: The Language of Love

Love. Ah, what a beautiful, elusive concept. It has been the topic of countless poems, songs, and novels. Love brings joy and fulfillment, but it can also bring pain and heartache. It is a language that we all yearn to understand and be fluent in. And just like any language, it has its own unique dialects. These dialects, or love languages, are the keys to unlocking the depth and intimacy of our relationships.

Over the years, as a Christian priest and counselor, I have had the privilege of witnessing numerous individuals struggling with issues related to love and relationships. From my experience, I can attest that understanding and speaking each other's love language is crucial for building genuine connections. In fact, it is like deciphering a secret code that helps us create a bridge between our hearts and the hearts of those we hold dear.

In his groundbreaking book, "The 5 Love Languages," Dr. Gary Chapman describes five distinct love languages through which individuals express and receive love. These love languages, namely words of affirmation, quality time, receiving gifts, acts of service, and physical touch, shape the way we experience and perceive love. Each individual resonates strongly with one or two of these languages, and when we speak their love language, we are effectively communicating our affection and care.

Take, for example, words of affirmation. Some individuals thrive on verbal appreciation and encouragement. Simple words such as "I love you" or "You mean the world to me" can fill their hearts with joy and reassurance. In contrast, quality time is the primary love language for others. These individuals value undivided attention and meaningful conversations. It is through spending quality time together, without distractions, that they feel loved and cherished.

Receiving gifts, acts of service, and physical touch are also powerful love languages, each conveying love in its own unique way. Some individuals treasure the thoughtfulness and effort behind a carefully chosen gift, while others deeply appreciate it when someone goes out of their way to help them with practical tasks. And then there are those who thrive on the power of touch, whether it be a gentle hug, a reassuring pat on the back, or simply holding hands.

Now imagine a husband whose love language is acts of service. Every day, he wakes up early to prepare breakfast for his wife, tidy up the house, and take care of mundane tasks. Yet his wife's primary love language is words of affirmation. She yearns to hear how much her husband loves and appreciates her. She longs to be affirmed for her hard work and dedication. In this scenario, despite the husband's best intentions, his acts of service may go unnoticed and fail to build the deep connection they both desire. However, if the wife takes the time to understand her husband's love language and reciprocate by expressing her love through acts of service, the couple will be able to communicate their affection in a way that resonates deeply with both of them. This understanding and effort to speak each other's love language unlocks the door to a more intimate and fulfilling relationship.

So, how do we unveil and speak the love language of those we care about? The first step is awareness. We must first recognize our own primary love language, as well as the love languages of those close to us. This can be done through observation and open communication. Pay attention to their words and actions, and listen to what they express appreciation for. Engage in heartfelt conversations about how they feel loved and how they express their love to others.

Once we have identified the love language of someone dear to us, the second step is to actively incorporate it into our daily interactions. This requires intentionality and effort. It may mean leaving sticky notes with words of affirmation for your partner, setting aside uninterrupted quality time with your children, surprising a friend with a small gift, or offering a comforting touch to someone in need. As we consistently speak each other's love languages, we will witness the transformational power it has in deepening our connections.

Understanding and speaking each other's love language is an ongoing journey, requiring patience, humility, and compassion. It is a dance of vulnerability, as we open ourselves up to language we may not be naturally fluent in. But as we take these steps to learn and grow, we will not only enhance the depth and intimacy of our relationships, but also experience the profound joy and fulfillment that comes

The Beauty of Random Acts of Kindness

In a world often consumed by self-interest and a fast-paced lifestyle, random acts of kindness serve as a gentle reminder of the beauty that exists in human nature. When we extend a helping hand to someone in need, whether it be a stranger or a loved one, we create a ripple effect that resonates far beyond the immediate act itself. A simple smile, a warm embrace, or a kind word can ignite a spark of hope, brightening even the darkest of days.

What makes these acts truly remarkable is their unpredictability. They are not bound by social norms or expectations, but are instead guided by a genuine desire to make someone else's life a little brighter. Whether it is buying a cup of coffee for the person behind us in line, offering a listening ear to a friend in distress, or volunteering at a local charity, these acts are spontaneous expressions of empathy and goodwill.

In fostering a sense of connection, empathy, and gratitude, random acts of kindness have the power to transform relationships. When we engage in these acts, we break down the barriers that often divide us, bridging the gap between strangers and friends, and deepening the bonds we share with loved ones. Through acts of kindness, we can build a network of support and trust, creating a strong foundation for authentic and lasting connections.

Moreover, random acts of kindness also serve as a reminder of our own blessings and the abundance of love in our lives. When we acknowledge the beauty in giving, we cultivate a spirit of gratitude that permeates through all aspects of our relationships. Gratitude allows us to appreciate and cherish the people around us, leading to a greater sense of fulfillment and joy.

Research has shown that acts of kindness not only benefit the recipient, but also have a positive impact on the giver. Engaging in these acts has been found to elevate mood, reduce stress levels, and promote overall well-being. It is in these moments of selflessness that we truly find ourselves and connect with our higher purpose.

As we journey through life, let us strive to make random acts of kindness a daily practice. Let us be the beacons of love and compassion that this world so desperately needs. In doing so, we not only foster a sense of connection and empathy in our relationships, but also create a ripple effect of kindness that has the potential to touch countless lives.

So, I invite you to join me on this soulful journey of building genuine relationships through the beauty of random acts of kindness. Together, let us create a world filled with love, compassion, and gratitude, one kind gesture at a time.

CHAPTER X

The Joy of Shared Experiences

The Magic of Adventure

There is a certain magic that comes alive when we embark on an adventure with others. It is in those moments of stepping out of our comfort zones that we discover our truest selves and forge deep connections with those we journey alongside. As a Christian priest and counselor, I have witnessed firsthand the transformative power of adventure, particularly when it comes to building genuine relationships.

In this chapter, we will dive into the realm of adventure and explore how venturing beyond our familiar territories can foster growth, create shared memories, and deepen connections. By embracing the unknown and taking risks together, we open ourselves up to a realm of possibility that can extend far beyond the boundaries of ordinary experiences.

1. The Threshold of Fear:

The first step towards embracing adventure is acknowledging and overcoming our fears. It is natural to feel apprehensive about stepping into the unknown, but it is also in those moments of fear that we can discover our inner strength. By venturing out of our comfort zones, whether it be through physical challenges or exploring new cultures and environments, we face our fears head-on. It is through these fearless experiences that we grow, not only individually but also in our relationships with others. Overcoming fear together creates a bond that is rooted in trust and mutual support, laying the foundation for authentic connections.

2. Growth Through Exploration:
Adventure is not merely about seeking adrenaline rushes and heart-pounding moments; it is about embracing personal growth. When we explore new horizons and push our boundaries, we are forced to confront our limitations and discover untapped potential within ourselves. As we navigate unfamiliar terrain, face unforeseen challenges, and adapt to new situations, we learn valuable life lessons. These personal transformations not only enrich our own lives but also create opportunities for connection and growth within our relationships. By witnessing and supporting each other's growth, we develop a deeper understanding and appreciation for one another.

3. Shared Memories:
One of the most beautiful aspects of embarking on adventures together is the creation of shared memories. Whether it be scaling a mountain peak, navigating uncharted waters, or even attempting a new recipe in the kitchen, these shared experiences become lasting memories that bind us together. These memories serve as touchstones in our relationships, evoking a sense of nostalgia and reminding us of the moments when we were truly alive. In times of joy, the memories of adventures past become celebrations of the incredible bonds we have formed with our companions.

4. Fostering Connection:
Adventure has a unique way of breaking down barriers and fostering connections that go beyond superficial interactions. When we navigate challenges together, relying on each other for support and guidance, we create a deep sense of camaraderie. The trust that is built through shared experiences allows us to be vulnerable and authentically ourselves. As we witness the triumphs and struggles of our fellow adventurers, we develop empathy and compassion, strengthening the fabric of our relationships. Adventure facilitates open and honest communication, creating a space where we can truly connect with one another.

Stepping outside of our comfort zones and embracing the unknown may initially seem daunting, but the rewards that come from these adventures are immeasurable. By taking risks together, we not only foster personal growth but also nurture genuine connections with those who choose to share in our journey. So let us embark on this magical adventure, weaving a tapestry of unforgettable memories and building soulful connections that will endure the test of time.

The Bond of Rituals

Rituals are more than just a sequence of actions; they symbolize a shared journey. They weave a tapestry of memories and experiences, creating a common thread that binds souls together. Rituals can range from simple daily routines to elaborate ceremonies, but their essence lies in the intentionality and presence we bring to them.

One of the most powerful aspects of rituals is their ability to provide a sense of stability and continuity in our ever-changing world. In a society where everything is constantly shifting and evolving, rituals ground us, reminding us of what is truly important. They serve as an anchor, a steady lighthouse amidst the storms of life. Whether it's a family dinner every Sunday evening or a morning prayer before starting the day, these rituals create a predictable rhythm that offers solace in times of chaos.

But rituals are not just about stability; they are also about creating moments of connection and joy. They hold the power to transform mundane activities into something sacred. Take, for example, the simple act of making a cup of tea together. Through the ritual of brewing tea, shared conversations unfold, hearts open, and a sense of togetherness blossoms. In this seemingly ordinary act, we find the extraordinary – the creation of a sacred space where relationships can flourish.

Research has supported the positive impact of rituals on relationships. Studies have shown that couples who engage in shared rituals experience higher relationship satisfaction and a sense of closeness. These rituals could be as simple as sharing a morning walk or a nightly bedtime routine. When we intentionally create rituals in our relationships, we are actively investing in the bond we share.

Moreover, rituals have the power to infuse our lives with deeper meaning. They remind us of our values, traditions, and the essence of who we are. Rituals can be an opportunity for introspection and self-discovery, fostering personal growth and transformation. By engaging in rituals, we honor our past, celebrate the present, and dream for the future.

To create meaningful rituals, we must first take the time to reflect on what truly matters to us. What values do we hold dear? What activities bring us joy and connect us with others? When we bring mindfulness and intentionality into our rituals, they become transformative experiences, elevating our relationships to new heights.

In conclusion, the bond of rituals is a potent force that can strengthen relationships, provide stability, and infuse everyday life with moments of connection and joy. As we embark on the journey of building genuine connections, let us not underestimate the power of intentional rituals. Let us embrace the simple and profound acts that bring us closer to one another, create a sense of stability, and fill our lives with sacred moments. May our souls dance to the rhythm of rituals, weaving a tapestry of love and authenticity.

CHAPTER XI

The Art of Mindful Communication

The Practice of Nonviolent Communication

Nonviolent communication is much more than a mere communication technique. It is a way of life, a philosophy rooted in empathy, understanding, and compassion. It is an approach that fosters soulful connections and allows individuals to engage in dialogue with one another, regardless of differences or conflicts. By deeply listening to others, acknowledging their needs, and expressing ourselves authentically, nonviolent communication opens doors for healing, growth, and meaningful dialogue.

In my experience, conflicts often arise due to the lack of effective communication and empathy. People tend to focus on their own needs and desires, neglecting to truly hear and understand the concerns of others. This leads to a breakdown in relationships, with unresolved conflicts festering beneath the surface. However, through the practice of nonviolent communication, individuals can learn to navigate these conflicts, ensuring that both parties feel heard and respected.

One of the foundational principles of nonviolent communication is the belief that all individuals have basic universal needs. These needs include physical well-being, safety, connection, autonomy, and significance. By recognizing and valuing these needs in ourselves and others, we can foster understanding and empathy. Rather than judging or blaming, nonviolent communication encourages us to approach conflicts with curiosity and a willingness to understand the underlying needs.

Through nonviolent communication, individuals are encouraged to express themselves authentically, using "I" statements to convey their feelings and needs. This approach allows for honest and open communication, without the room for defensiveness or blame. Additionally, when conflicts arise, nonviolent communication emphasizes the importance of active listening. This means truly hearing and understanding the other person's perspective, without interrupting or formulating a response.

Creating a safe space for open and honest communication is essential for building genuine relationships. Nonviolent communication provides a framework for establishing this safe space, where individuals feel free to express themselves without fear of judgment or rejection. This practice fosters trust and vulnerability, allowing for deeper connections to be formed.

In my work with school and college students, I have witnessed firsthand the positive impact of nonviolent communication. By learning the principles of empathy and active listening, students have been able to resolve conflicts in healthier ways. It has facilitated stronger bonds within peer groups, leading to a more positive and inclusive environment.

Similarly, in times of crisis, nonviolent communication has provided a lifeline for individuals struggling with grief, trauma, or relationship difficulties. By creating a safe space for expression, it has enabled people to navigate their emotions and find solace in connection. Nonviolent communication has been instrumental in helping individuals rebuild fractured relationships, heal emotional wounds, and ultimately find inner peace.

As I continue to delve deeper into the art of building genuine relationships, I firmly believe that the practice of nonviolent communication is a crucial aspect. It not only helps to resolve conflicts and improve understanding but also cultivates empathy, compassion, and a sense of collective responsibility. By embracing nonviolent communication, we can create a more harmonious world, one soulful connection at a time.

The Power of Silence

In this fast-paced world, where noise and distractions incessantly surround us, it's easy to overlook the profound influence of silence. We often perceive silence as an absence of sound, a void waiting to be filled. But what if we shift our perspective and embrace silence as an opportunity for connection, reflection, and understanding?

One of the fundamental aspects of effective communication is active listening. It is through attentive listening that we truly comprehend the thoughts, feelings, and desires of others. However, we often find ourselves caught up in the urge to respond, offering opinions or advice, as if silence were an inconvenience.

But what if, instead of rushing to fill the silence, we allowed it to permeate the space between us? What if we sat in silence, giving the other person the time and space they need to process their thoughts and articulate their feelings?

Silence has the power to create a safe and non-judgmental environment, allowing individuals to explore the depths of their emotions and share their innermost struggles. It is in these moments of silence that true connection can be established, as we offer a sanctuary for vulnerability and honesty.

Embracing moments of silence also provides an opportunity for reflection. In a culture that values action and external achievements, we often neglect the importance of self-reflection. However, it is in moments of silence that we can delve deep into our inner worlds, examining our own motivations, fears, and aspirations.

By incorporating silence into our interactions, we create a space for introspection and self-exploration. This, in turn, allows us to gain a deeper understanding of ourselves and others, fostering empathy and compassion within our relationships.

Moreover, silence allows for the possibility of experiencing a profound sense of connection beyond words. In silence, we tap into a realm where words become limitations, and a profound understanding can be forged in the absence of verbal communication. It is through silent moments that we can truly hear the unspoken desires, hopes, and pains of the soul.

However, it is important to note that the power of silence should not be misunderstood as a complete absence of communication. Silence is not to be equated with isolation or withdrawal. It is about creating space within conversations, allowing each individual to be fully heard and understood.

As I have journeyed with individuals facing various crises, I have come to realize that embracing silence requires practice, intention, and patience. It necessitates being comfortable with the discomfort and allowing the silence to speak its own language.

In conclusion, the power of silence in building genuine relationships cannot be denied. As we learn to embrace silence, we unlock a realm of connection, reflection, and understanding previously unexplored. So, let us venture forth, willing to create space for silence in our conversations and experiences, for it is in the depths of silence that true soulful connections are forged.

CHAPTER XII

The Enchantment of Serendipity

Embracing Chance Encounters

As I reflect upon my many years as a Christian priest and counselor, it becomes abundantly clear that some of the most transformative moments in our lives come from encounters we never expected. These serendipitous meetings, these beautiful chance encounters, hold within them the potential to bring about genuine and lasting connections.

In a world that often feels preoccupied with planned meetings and purposeful connections, we tend to overlook the spontaneous magic that can occur when our paths intersect with someone we had no intention of meeting. These are the moments that remind us of the beauty in surrendering to the unknown and embracing the unforeseen opportunities that life presents.

One case study that comes to mind vividly is the story of Joice, a young woman I had the privilege of counseling during her years in college. Joice, a highly introverted and reserved individual, had always struggled with forming meaningful relationships. She found solace in solitude, often finding herself curled up with a book in the quiet corners of the campus library. However, fate had a different plan in store for her.

On a sunny afternoon, Joice decided to venture out of her comfort zone and attend a poetry reading at a local book store. Little did she know that this simple act of spontaneity would forever change the course of her life. As she sat there, absorbed in the soulful words being spoken, she found herself captivated by the presence of a complete stranger.

Luke, a vibrant and charismatic artist, approached Joice during the intermission, drawn to her quiet demeanor amidst the animated crowd. Their conversation flowed effortlessly, as if they had known each other for years. It was in that moment, that chance encounter, that a genuine connection began to blossom.

From that day forward, their lives became entangled in a beautiful dance of shared experiences and deep soul connections. Luke opened Joice's eyes to a world of creativity and self-expression, while Joice became Luke's constant source of grounding and support. Their chance encounter not only challenged Joice's preconceived notions of relationships but also ignited a fire within her to embrace the unknown and welcome the spontaneous opportunities that life had to offer.

Joice's story is just one of the many examples I have witnessed throughout my own journey as a counselor. Time and time again, I have seen the transformative power of these serendipitous connections. It is through embracing chance encounters that we are able to break down the walls we have built around ourselves and truly allow others to touch our souls.

Research supports the idea that chance encounters can have a profound impact on our lives. In a study conducted by psychologists at the University of California, participants were asked to reflect on significant events in their lives and identify which ones were chance encounters. The results showed that these unplanned meetings were often considered to be the most meaningful and influential moments.

So how can we actively embrace chance encounters and open ourselves up to the potential for genuine connections? It starts with cultivating a mindset of openness and curiosity, letting go of the need for control and embracing the uncertainty that comes with unexpected meetings. We must learn to listen to the whispers of our intuition and be present in every moment, for it is in these moments that we may stumble upon the very connections that our souls have been yearning for.

In the art of building genuine relationships, chance encounters hold a special place. They remind us that the universe has a way of orchestrating beautiful moments of connection, even amidst the chaos of our everyday lives. So let us be open to the possibility of serendipity and embrace the unexpected with open hearts, for you never know where your next chance encounter may lead you.

The Power of Synchronicity

My dear readers, have you ever experienced a moment in your life when it felt like everything was falling into place? A moment when the universe seemed to align itself in a way that left you in awe? These moments, my friends, are not mere coincidences; they are profound manifestations of synchronicity.

Synchronicity, a term coined by the renowned psychologist Carl Jung, refers to the meaningful coincidences that occur in our lives. It is as if the universe is conspiring to bring the right people, experiences, and opportunities into our path, guiding us toward our purpose and the connections we are meant to make.

I have witnessed the power of synchronicity time and time again in my work as a counselor and Christian priest. One particular case comes to mind – the story of Feba, a college student who was struggling to find her place in the world and build meaningful relationships. Feba had always felt like an outsider, unable to connect deeply with those around her. She longed for a tribe, a community where she could truly belong.

During our counseling sessions, I introduced Feba to the concept of synchronicity and encouraged her to pay attention to the signs and coincidences that were unfolding in her life. We embarked on a journey of exploration, encouraging her to be open and receptive to the universe's subtle whispers.

One day, as Feba was walking through her college campus feeling particularly lonely, she noticed a flyer hanging on the bulletin board. It was an advertisement for a student-led spirituality group that was seeking new members. Intrigued, Feba decided to attend their next meeting, hoping that it might provide her with the sense of community she had been searching for.

Little did she know, this decision would change the course of her life forever. As she walked into that small classroom, she was greeted by a group of warm and accepting individuals who shared her values and beliefs. Through their shared spiritual practices, discussions, and support, Feba found herself not only forming deep connections but also discovering her own spiritual path – one that resonated with her soul.

The synchronicity did not end there. Through her newfound tribe, Feba was introduced to an older woman named Grace, who happened to be searching for a mentor for a group of young women at a local hostel. Feba, remembering her own struggles with loneliness and the power of finding her tribe, jumped at the opportunity to help guide these young women on their own journeys.

As Feba immersed herself in this new role, she realized that her experiences of feeling like an outsider had given her a unique perspective and empathy that allowed her to connect deeply with these young women. Together, they formed a bond of trust and understanding, transforming their lives and the lives of those around them.

Feba's story serves as a testament to the profound impact that synchronicity can have on our lives. It reminds us to be open to the signs and coincidences that unfold, for they are not random occurrences but guideposts on our journey towards building soulful connections and finding our tribe.

Dear readers, I encourage you to reflect on the moments of synchronicity that have graced your own life. What were the meaningful coincidences that led you to soulful connections and a sense of belonging? Embrace these moments and trust in the power of the universe to bring the right people into your life at the right time.

Remember, building genuine relationships is not a solitary pursuit; it is a dance of synchronicity, where the universe orchestrates the meeting of souls. So, let us open our hearts, minds, and spirits to the magic of synchronicity, for it is through these meaningful coincidences that we can truly find our tribe and forge soulful connections that transcend time and space.

Creating Space for Serendipity

In our fast-paced world, it is easy to become consumed by our daily responsibilities and commitments, leaving little room for spontaneity. We are constantly rushing from one task to another, rarely taking the time to pause and truly experience the present moment. But what if we consciously made an effort to create space in our lives for serendipity to occur? What if we welcomed the unexpected with open hearts and open minds?

The key to fostering serendipity lies in cultivating an open mindset. It starts with acknowledging that not everything in life can be planned and controlled. By embracing the uncertainty of the unknown, we open ourselves up to a world of possibilities. We become more attuned to the subtle signs of serendipity, those fleeting moments of connection that can transform our lives.

Creating space for serendipity also requires us to let go of our preconceived notions and expectations. Often, we enter into conversations and interactions with a specific outcome in mind. We hope to network, impress, or achieve a certain goal. However, when we approach relationships with rigid intentions, we inadvertently limit the potential for genuine connections. Instead, we must release our attachments to specific outcomes and be present in the moment, allowing for the magic of serendipity to unfold.

One practical way to invite serendipitous moments into our lives is by stepping outside of our comfort zones. We must be willing to explore the unfamiliar and engage with people from different backgrounds and perspectives. By venturing beyond our social bubbles, we expose ourselves to a myriad of opportunities for serendipitous encounters. We may strike up a conversation with a stranger in a coffee shop, attend a community event, or join a new club or organization. Through these interactions, we give serendipity the chance to work its wonders.

Another essential aspect of creating space for serendipity is being fully present in our interactions. How often have we found ourselves engaged in a conversation, only to be mentally preoccupied with our endless to-do lists or upcoming plans? When we are not fully present, we miss out on the subtle cues and signals that can lead to transformative connections. By practicing mindfulness and grounding ourselves in the present moment, we become more attuned to the nuances of human interaction, allowing serendipity to weave its magic.

Finally, we must learn to embrace the beauty of the unexpected. Serendipity often manifests itself through chance encounters, unplanned detours, and unforeseen circumstances. It is in those spontaneous moments that we have the opportunity to forge meaningful connections with others. Rather than resisting or fearing the unexpected, we must lean into it with an open heart and open mind. By doing so, we create the ideal conditions for serendipitous relationships to blossom.

In conclusion, cultivating an open mindset and creating space in our lives for serendipity is crucial for building genuine relationships. By releasing our attachments to specific outcomes, stepping outside of our comfort zones, being fully present, and embracing the unexpected, we invite serendipitous moments into our lives. These moments, often small and seemingly insignificant, have the potential to transform our lives and forge deep connections with others. So, let us be open, let us be present, and let us welcome the delightful surprises that serendipity has in store for us.

CHAPTER XIII

The Dance of Vulnerability

The Courage to Be Seen

To explore the depth of this topic, let us delve into the story of Aditi, a young woman who approached me during a particularly tumultuous time in her life. Aditi, a recent college graduate, found herself engulfed in darkness, unable to decipher her own emotions and longing for a sense of connection. Through our conversations, it became evident that Aditi's struggle stemmed from a fear of being seen for who she truly was.

Aditi had mastered the art of hiding, adorning herself with a carefully constructed facade of confidence and contentment. Behind that mask, however, lay a sense of emptiness and fear that had been intricately woven into the tapestry of her life. Her fear of rejection and judgment outweighed her desire to be authentic, leading her to guard her true self from the world.

Deep within her soul, Aditi yearned to be seen and loved for who she truly was. Yet, the very thought of exposing her vulnerabilities and imperfections incited a paralyzing fear within her. She believed that if she allowed herself to be seen in her entirety, she would be met with rejection and disappointment. This belief had rooted itself within her being, hindering her relationships and creating a barrier to genuine connection.

Together, we embarked on a journey of self-discovery and vulnerability. I encouraged Aditi to acknowledge her fear and face it head-on. We explored the beauty that lay hidden within her imperfections and the strength that vulnerability could bring to her relationships. It was not an easy path, but as Aditi began to shed the layers of her perceived perfection, she discovered a newfound sense of freedom and authenticity.

It was through her willingness to be seen that Aditi found solace and healing. She learned that true connection can only occur when we have the courage to show up as our authentic selves. Aditi's willingness to let go of the fear of judgment allowed her to create genuine connections, where she felt accepted and loved for who she truly was. In embracing her vulnerabilities, she unveiled a strength that shone brightly, captivating those around her with the raw beauty of her soul.

Aditi's story serves as a reminder to all of us that courage lies within each one of us, waiting to be harnessed. It is through the vulnerability of showing up as our authentic selves that we find true connection and build genuine relationships. The courage to be seen requires us to confront our fears head-on, to embrace our imperfections, and to allow ourselves to be loved for who we truly are.

Let us now embark on a journey together, exploring the depths of vulnerability and the power it holds in forging soulful connections. As we delve into the intricacies of building genuine relationships, may the stories shared and insights gained inspire us to embrace our authentic selves, to be seen, and to experience the beauty and strength that vulnerability brings.

Embracing Imperfections

In today's social media-driven society, where carefully curated images and polished personas dominate our online presence, it is tempting to believe that perfection is the ultimate goal. We strive to be flawless, to present ourselves as the person we believe others want us to be. But in doing so, we deny ourselves and others the opportunity to truly connect on a deeper level.

I have seen countless individuals, burdened by their own perceived flaws and imperfections, desperate for acceptance. They hide behind a well-constructed facade, frightened that their vulnerabilities will be met with judgement and rejection. Yet, what they fail to realize is that it is through our imperfections that we find our true strength and pave the way for authentic connections.

Learning to embrace imperfections begins with self-acceptance. It requires a shift in mindset, a breaking free from the shackles of societal expectations. It means understanding that we are all flawed, and that it is these flaws that make us unique and relatable. As I have counseled numerous students and those going through crisis, I have witnessed the transformative power of self-acceptance. When we let go of the need to present a flawless image, we open ourselves up to genuine connections and draw others towards us.

But embracing imperfections does not end with ourselves; it extends to those we encounter in our lives. When we approach others with an open heart and mind, ready to accept them for who they truly are, imperfections and all, we create an environment where genuine connections can thrive. For it is in vulnerability that true intimacy is born, and it is in imperfection that trust is forged.

I have seen this truth play out time and time again in my work with students and those navigating through crisis. When individuals feel safe and supported in embracing their flaws, they are able to open up and share their deepest struggles and desires. In doing so, they establish a bond built on genuine understanding and compassion.

In a world that often tells us that perfection is the key to happiness and connection, we must remember that it is in our imperfections that the true essence of life resides. It is through our struggles and vulnerabilities that we grow, learn, and connect with others on a profound level. As we learn to embrace imperfections, both in ourselves and in those around us, we create a ripple effect, spreading acceptance and genuine connection throughout our communities.

So, let us dare to be imperfect. Let us embrace the cracks and flaws that make us who we are. For it is in these imperfections that we find our truest selves and build the most profound connections.

The Healing Power of Vulnerability

As I sit down to write about the healing power of vulnerability, my mind is flooded with memories of the countless individuals I have encountered on my journey as a Christian priest and counselor. People from all walks of life, going through various trials and tribulations, seeking solace and guidance. And in each of these encounters, one common thread stands out – the transformative impact of vulnerability in forging deep emotional connections and creating a safe space for healing and growth.

In a world that often encourages us to put on a façade of strength and invulnerability, it can be daunting to expose our true selves to others. We fear judgment, rejection, and the possibility of being hurt. Yet, it is through vulnerability that we allow others to see us for who we truly are and invite them into our inner world. It is through vulnerability that we open ourselves up to the possibility of genuine connection and healing.

Research studies have consistently shown that vulnerability plays a crucial role in building authentic relationships. In fact, the renowned Brené Brown, who has extensively researched vulnerability, describes it as the birthplace of love, belonging, joy, courage, empathy, and creativity. Through her work, she reveals that vulnerability is not a sign of weakness, but rather an act of immense strength and courage.

When we allow ourselves to be vulnerable, we create a safe space for others to reciprocate and share their own struggles and fears. This reciprocity deepens the bond between individuals, fostering a profound sense of trust and understanding. It is within this space that healing can take place, as both parties find solace and support in knowing that they are not alone in their experiences.

Furthermore, vulnerability enables us to express our emotional needs and desires openly and honestly. By doing so, we invite others to meet us where we are and provide the necessary emotional support. In turn, this cultivates mutual growth and personal development, as we learn from each other's perspectives and experiences.

However, it is important to note that vulnerability must be nurtured in a safe and supportive environment. It requires both individuals to show empathy, compassion, and sensitivity towards each other's vulnerabilities. It is a delicate dance that requires communication, understanding, and a genuine willingness to listen and validate one another. Only then can vulnerability truly flourish and lead to healing within the relationship.

To uncover the healing power of vulnerability, it is essential to let go of the fear of judgment and rejection. Embrace your unique experiences, emotions, and vulnerabilities, for they are what make you authentically you. Remember that vulnerability is a strength, not a weakness. It takes courage to share your deepest truths with another person, but it is through this act of courage that you create space for profound emotional connections and personal growth.

In the upcoming chapters, we will explore practical strategies and exercises that can help you cultivate vulnerability within your relationships. From mindful listening to practicing self-compassion, these tools will empower you to forge deeper connections and create a safe space for healing and growth. Together, we will embark on a transformative journey towards building soulful connections through the power of vulnerability.

CHAPTER XIV

The Art of Soulful Listening

The Power of Silence

As a Christian Priest and Counselor, I have spent countless hours interacting with people from all walks of life. From school and college students to individuals in the midst of personal crisis, I have witnessed firsthand the struggles we face in building genuine relationships. It is in these moments of connection and vulnerability that I have come to appreciate the transformative power of silence in communication.

In our fast-paced and noisy world, we often underestimate the value of silence in fostering deeper connections. We are conditioned to believe that meaningful communication involves constant verbal exchange and expression. However, silence holds a sacred space that words alone cannot penetrate. It is in this silence that we can truly listen, not just to the words being spoken, but to the unspoken emotions and desires that lie beneath the surface.

Creating space for silence requires intention and practice. It begins by cultivating a deep sense of presence and mindfulness. When engaged in conversation, instead of anxiously awaiting our turn to speak, we can choose to really hear the other person, to honor their experiences and emotions. By doing so, we create an environment where silence is welcomed and encouraged, a place where true understanding can emerge.

Silence allows for introspection, giving individuals the opportunity to delve into their own thoughts and emotions. In the midst of a conversation, a well-timed pause can offer a moment of reflection and clarity. It is through this silence that we can process information, untangle complex emotions, and truly understand ourselves and others.

Beyond introspection, silence also creates space for empathy and connection. When we pause and truly listen, we open ourselves up to the experiences and perspectives of others. Without the pressure to respond immediately, we can fully absorb their stories, concerns, and joys. This deep listening acknowledges the value and worth of the other person, building a bridge of empathy and understanding.

Silence can also serve as a powerful tool in resolving conflicts and navigating difficult conversations. Often, during moments of disagreement or tension, our instinct may be to argue or defend our positions. However, by embracing silence as an integral part of the conversation, we can diffuse hostility and create an atmosphere of cooperation and respect. When we allow silence to exist, we invite the other person to share their thoughts without fear of interruption or judgment. This paves the way for genuine dialogue, where both parties can express their perspectives and work towards resolution.

In our journey towards building soulful connections, we must recognize the profound impact that silence can have on our communication. By intentionally creating space for silence, we unlock the transformative power that lies within. In doing so, we honor the sacredness of each person's story and create a safe haven for true understanding and connection to flourish. Let us embrace the beauty of silence and allow it to guide us on our path towards building genuine relationships.

The Language of Presence

In my years as a Christian Priest and Counselor, I have witnessed the power of presence in building genuine relationships. It is a language that transcends words, a profound way of connecting with others on a deeper level. To truly understand the language of presence, we must first delve into its definition and context.

Presence, in its essence, is the state of being fully engaged and attentive to the present moment. It involves listening intently, not just with our ears, but with our entire being. This means being aware of the other person's body language, facial expressions, and emotions. It requires us to set aside our own distractions and concerns, and be completely present with the other person.

When we communicate beyond words, we tap into the unspoken and subtle aspects of human connection. We sense the emotions that lie beneath the surface, and we respond not just to what is said, but to what is implied. This kind of communication requires a deep level of empathy and vulnerability, as we open ourselves to truly understanding and being understood.

The language of presence is not just about being physically present; it is also about creating a safe and welcoming space for others to share their thoughts and emotions. It is about giving our full attention and showing genuine interest in what the other person has to say. When we practice the art of being fully present, we validate the experiences and feelings of others, and we build trust and connection.

But how do we cultivate this language of presence? It starts with a willingness to let go of our own agenda and ego, and to truly prioritize the well-being of the other person. It requires us to let go of our judgments and assumptions, and to approach every interaction with an open mind and heart.

One of the key elements of the language of presence is active listening. It involves not just hearing what the other person is saying, but also understanding the underlying emotions and desires. This kind of listening goes beyond words; it involves paying attention to nonverbal cues, such as body language and tone of voice. It requires us to be fully engaged and focused solely on the person in front of us.

When we truly listen, we validate the other person's experiences and emotions. We create a space for them to be vulnerable and authentic, and we show them that they are seen and heard. This kind of presence can be transformative, as it allows for deep connections to be formed and for healing to take place.

The language of presence is not limited to verbal communication; it also encompasses our actions and behaviors. It is about showing up for others consistently and compassionately, and demonstrating through our actions that we value and care for them. It involves being reliable, trustworthy, and responsive to the needs of others.

In a world that is often filled with distractions and noise, the language of presence is a powerful tool for creating soulful connections. It requires us to slow down, to be fully present, and to listen with all our senses. When we embrace this language, we open ourselves to the beauty and depth of human connection, and we invite others to do the same.

So, I invite you to dive into the language of presence.

Explore its nuances and practice the art of being fully present with others. Cultivate empathy, active listening, and compassionate actions. Discover the transformative power of connecting beyond words, and experience the joy and fulfillment that comes from building genuine relationships.

Empathy in Action

As I have walked alongside countless individuals in my role as a Christian priest and counselor, I have witnessed the profound impact that empathy can have on building genuine connections. It is a key ingredient that allows us to truly understand and connect with others on a deeper level.

Empathy is not just about feeling sorry for someone or expressing understanding from a distance. It goes beyond that. It involves stepping into someone else's shoes, fully immersing ourselves in their world, and genuinely seeking to understand their perspective. It is an active and intentional effort to connect with others on an emotional and psychological level.

In today's fast-paced and increasingly disconnected world, empathy stands as a beacon of light, reminding us of our shared humanity and the power of understanding. It is through empathy that we can bridge the gaps that divide us, dissolve misconceptions, and build lasting connections.

To unleash the power of empathy in building genuine connections, we must first cultivate a deep sense of self-awareness. We need to become attuned to our own emotions, biases, and judgments, recognizing that they can shape our perceptions and interactions with others. By acknowledging our own limitations, we open ourselves up to truly hearing and understanding the experiences of others.

The next step is to actively listen. True empathy requires us to be fully present, setting aside our own agendas and distractions. It means giving our undivided attention to the person in front of us, listening not only to their words but also to their emotions and nonverbal cues. By doing so, we can pick up on subtle nuances that reveal their true feelings and experiences.

Empathy also involves practicing perspective-taking. It is about putting ourselves in someone else's shoes and imagining what it must be like to walk in their world. This act of imagination allows us to gain a deeper understanding of their struggles, joys, and fears. It enables us to move beyond our own limited worldview and embrace the richness and diversity that exists within humanity.

But empathy does not end with understanding. It compels us to respond with compassion and understanding. It drives us to take action in ways that support and uplift others. Whether it's offering a word of encouragement, providing a helping hand, or simply being there to listen, our empathy transforms into tangible gestures of care and support.

Research has shown that empathy has a reciprocal effect. When we extend empathy to others, not only do we forge deeper connections, but we also experience personal growth and fulfillment. It nurtures a sense of purpose and belonging within us, reminding us of the interconnectedness that binds us all.

In a world that often feels divided and detached, the power of empathy to build genuine connections is needed now more than ever. It is a powerful tool that has the potential to heal wounds, foster understanding, and create a more compassionate society.

So, let us embark on this journey of empathy in action. Let us commit to stepping outside of ourselves, embracing the perspectives of others, and responding with compassion and understanding. In doing so, we will not only enhance our own lives, but also contribute to a world where genuine connections flourish.

CHAPTER XV

The Magic of Rituals and Traditions

Creating Meaningful Rituals

In the hustle and bustle of modern life, it is easy to lose sight of the importance of rituals. We often rush through our daily routines without really pausing to consider their significance. However, rituals have the power to transform our relationships, infusing them with love, joy, and a deep sense of connection. As a Christian Priest and Counselor with many years of experience working with individuals in various stages of life, I have witnessed firsthand the transformative impact that intentional rituals can have on relationships. In this chapter, we will explore the art of creating meaningful rituals and discover how they can bring joy and a sense of belonging into our everyday lives.

The first step in creating meaningful rituals is to recognize the power of intentionality. Rituals are not mere routines or habits; they are purposeful actions that carry deep meaning and symbolism. Whether it is a morning routine, a weekly family dinner, or a yearly holiday tradition, each ritual should be infused with intention and significance. By consciously choosing to engage in these rituals, we are acknowledging and affirming the importance of our relationships, thereby fostering connection at a deeper level.

To begin this journey of creating meaningful rituals, it is helpful to start with an exploration of our own values, beliefs, and aspirations. Consider what matters most to you and your loved ones. What values and principles do you hold dear? What are the shared beliefs and goals that bind your relationships together? Reflecting on these questions will help you identify the themes and elements that can be woven into your rituals, making them truly meaningful and authentic.

Once you have identified the core values and beliefs that underpin your relationships, the next step is to translate them into tangible actions. Rituals can take on many forms, from simple daily practices to grand annual celebrations. The key is to choose activities that resonate with you and your loved ones. For example, if family togetherness is a cherished value, you might establish a weekly family game night, where everyone gathers to play games, share stories, and simply enjoy each other's company. If gratitude is an important principle in your relationships, consider starting a daily gratitude practice, where family members take turns expressing gratitude for something they appreciate about one another.

In addition to incorporating your core values and beliefs, it is equally important to honor the individuality of each person in your relationships. Rituals should be inclusive and meaningful to all parties involved. Allow each person to contribute their ideas and preferences, creating a sense of ownership and investment in the rituals. By doing so, you are affirming the uniqueness and significance of each individual, strengthening the bonds of connection and fostering a sense of belonging.

Finally, remember that meaningful rituals are not set in stone. They evolve and adapt alongside your relationships. Allow room for flexibility and growth, encouraging open dialogue and feedback. As life circumstances change and new challenges arise, rituals might need to be adjusted or even replaced. The key is to approach these changes with grace and openness, viewing them as an opportunity for deeper connection rather than a disruption to the status quo.

Creating meaningful rituals is an ongoing process, one that requires time, effort, and a genuine desire to foster connection. As you embark on this journey, be patient with yourself and your loved ones. Remember that the most important aspect of any ritual is the love and intention behind it. By infusing your daily lives with intentional rituals, you will deepen your relationships, bring joy into your interactions, and create a lasting sense of belonging. This chapter will provide you with guidance and inspiration as you embark on this transformative journey.

Embracing Cultural Traditions

As I delve into the topic of embracing cultural traditions, I am reminded of the countless encounters I have had with individuals from various cultural backgrounds. Each interaction has left an indelible mark on my soul, opening my eyes to the richness and beauty that lies within the diverse tapestry of human customs and rituals.

In a world that is becoming increasingly interconnected, it is crucial that we make a conscious effort to bridge the gaps between different cultures. By embracing and celebrating cultural traditions, we not only foster understanding between individuals, but we also create a sense of unity and inclusivity that transcends boundaries.

In my years as a Christian priest and counselor, I have witnessed firsthand how cultural traditions can serve as a powerful tool in breaking down barriers and fostering meaningful connections. Whether it is through music, dance, art, language, or cuisine, every cultural tradition encapsulates a unique expression of identity and heritage.

One of the greatest joys of embracing cultural traditions is the opportunity to explore the vast array of customs from around the world. Each tradition holds within it a treasure trove of stories, values, and wisdom passed down through generations. By immersing ourselves in these traditions, we gain a deeper understanding of the people who practice them and the experiences that shape their lives.

For instance, I recall an encounter with a young student who had recently moved to our city from a rural village in India. Feeling out of place and disconnected from her roots, she was struggling to find her identity in the midst of a foreign culture. As we sat together, I encouraged her to share her cultural traditions and rituals with me. Through her stories, I learned about the vibrant festivals celebrated in her village, the intricate designs of her traditional clothing, and the songs that echoed through her community during special occasions.

Together, we embarked on a journey to rediscover the beauty of her cultural heritage. We delved into the history behind her traditions, learning about the significance of each ritual and the values it upheld. In the process, I witnessed an incredible transformation within her. As she began to embrace her cultural traditions, she found a renewed sense of pride in her identity and a newfound confidence in navigating the complexities of her new environment.

Embracing cultural traditions is not only about understanding and appreciating the customs of others, but also about celebrating our own. When we take the time to reflect on our own cultural heritage, we gain a deeper understanding of ourselves and the values that have been instilled within us from a young age.

By embracing our own traditions and sharing them with others, we become ambassadors of our culture, weaving a tapestry of understanding and respect. It is through these shared experiences that the gaps between individuals are bridged, fostering a sense of unity that transcends superficial differences.

In conclusion, embracing cultural traditions is a powerful tool in building genuine relationships. By exploring and appreciating the customs and rituals of diverse cultures, we gain a deeper understanding of others and foster unity in a world that is often divided. As we celebrate our own traditions and share them with others, we create a space where cultural differences are not only accepted but celebrated. May we all find the courage to embrace the richness of cultural traditions and build bridges of understanding and connection in our own lives.

CHAPTER XVI

The Power of Forgiveness and Healing

The Path to Forgiveness

As I sit down to write about the path to forgiveness, I am reminded of the countless individuals I have counseled over the years. Each person had their own unique story of pain, betrayal, and heartache that led them to me seeking solace and guidance. Forgiveness, I have learned, is not a simple task; it is a journey that requires patience, understanding, and a willingness to let go.

In this chapter, I invite you to join me on this path to forgiveness, as we explore how to release resentment and embrace compassion. Together, we will uncover the immense power forgiveness holds for personal growth and healing, and how it grants us the freedom to let go of past hurts.

Step 1: Acknowledge and Validate Your Feelings

Initiating the journey towards forgiveness begins with acknowledging and validating your feelings. It is essential to recognize the pain and anger that resides within you. As humans, it is natural for us to feel hurt when we have been wronged, betrayed, or harmed. By acknowledging these emotions, you honor your truth and grant yourself permission to heal.

Step 2: Reflect and Understand

Once you have acknowledged your feelings, the next step is to reflect and understand the root causes of the pain. Take the time to delve deep within yourself and explore your beliefs, expectations, and desires that were shattered by the hurtful actions of others. This introspection allows you to gain a greater understanding of the situation and the impact it had on you.

Step 3: Shift Perspectives and Cultivate Empathy

Shifting perspectives and cultivating empathy is a crucial step on the path to forgiveness. This means placing yourself in the shoes of the person who hurt you and trying to understand their motivations, fears, and struggles. It does not mean condoning their behavior or excusing their actions, but rather seeking to comprehend them on a deeper level. Empathy opens the door to compassion, helping us recognize the humanity in others and find a common ground for forgiveness.

Step 4: Set Boundaries and Protect Yourself

While forgiveness is a powerful tool for personal growth and healing, it does not mean subjecting yourself to further harm or allowing others to continue to mistreat you. Setting boundaries is an integral part of the forgiveness process. It means recognizing your worth and protecting yourself from future hurt. By establishing healthy boundaries, you create a safe space for both yourself and others to grow and heal.

Step 5: Practice Self-Compassion and Self-Forgiveness

On the path to forgiveness, it is crucial to extend the same compassion and forgiveness to ourselves as we do to others.

We are all prone to making mistakes, and it is essential to recognize our own fallibility. Practice self-compassion by offering understanding and forgiveness to yourself for any perceived wrongdoings or shortcomings. Embrace the healing power of self-forgiveness, allowing it to uplift and guide you towards a place of inner peace.

Step 6: Release Resentment and Let Go

The final step on the path to forgiveness is to release resentment and let go. Holding onto anger, resentment, and grudges only serves to weigh us down and hinder our personal growth. By choosing to let go, we free ourselves from the chains of bitterness and open our hearts to a more profound sense of peace and liberation.

As you embark on this journey to forgiveness, remember that it is not a linear process. There will be days when the pain feels overwhelming, and forgiveness seems impossible. Be patient and gentle with yourself. Healing takes time, and each step forward brings you closer to the transformative power of forgiveness.

In the chapters that follow, I will share stories of individuals who have walked this path and emerged stronger and more resilient. Through their experiences, we will gain insights into the power of forgiveness in cultivating genuine relationships and fostering soulful connections.

Join me as we embark on this transformative journey of forgiveness, for it is through forgiveness that we can truly embrace the art of building genuine relationships and find the profound connection that our souls crave.

Healing Wounds, Restoring Connections

Understanding the Process of Healing

In the journey of building genuine relationships, there are bound to be moments of hurt, disappointment, and betrayal. These wounds, if left unaddressed, can fester and erode the trust and connection between individuals. However, through the art of healing, we have the opportunity to restore those connections and create something even stronger and more resilient.

As a Christian Priest and Counselor, I have had the privilege of working with individuals from diverse backgrounds – from school and college students to people going through personal crises. One thing that has become abundantly clear in all these interactions is the inherent power of healing wounds in repairing and rebuilding relationships.

But what does the process of healing entail? It begins with acknowledging the wounds that exist and bravely facing the pain associated with them. Many times, we might be tempted to push painful memories deep within ourselves, hoping that time alone will heal our wounds. However, healing requires a conscious decision to confront and feel the emotions tied to those wounds.

Research has shown that when we allow ourselves to experience and process these emotions rather than suppressing them, we pave the way for true healing to take place. This process can be challenging and unsettling, but it is also incredibly liberating. By uncovering the raw and often vulnerable parts of ourselves, we are able to make space for healing and restoration to occur.

Repairing Trust in Relationships

One of the most significant casualties of broken connections is trust. When trust is shattered, it can be difficult to imagine rebuilding it. However, I firmly believe that trust can be repaired, and the process of healing plays a vital role in this restoration.

To repair trust, the first step is to create a safe and non-judgmental space for open communication. Both parties must be willing to listen and understand each other's perspectives without jumping to conclusions or laying blame. This requires vulnerability and humility, as genuine healing cannot occur without acknowledging our own contributions to the breakdown of trust.

In addition, rebuilding trust requires consistency and follow-through. It is not enough to simply apologize and promise change; actions must align with words. Small acts of kindness, honesty, and reliability over time can slowly rebuild the trust that was lost.

Rebuilding Broken Bonds

When relationships suffer from deep wounds, it often feels like the bond between individuals has been irreparably damaged. However, I have witnessed firsthand the incredible resilience of human connections and the power of healing to not only mend broken bonds but to create something even stronger than before.

Rebuilding broken bonds begins with forgiveness. This is not to say that we should brush aside the pain or forget the events that led to the fracture. Rather, forgiveness is about releasing ourselves from the burden of carrying resentment and allowing ourselves to move forward. It is an act of self-liberation that opens up the possibility for genuine reconciliation.

When both parties are committed to the process of healing, rebuilding broken bonds becomes a collaborative effort. It requires open communication, empathy, and a willingness to learn from past mistakes. It entails understanding each other's needs, values, and fears, and actively working towards meeting those needs with compassion and understanding.

As connections are rebuilt, it is essential to remember that healing takes time. Patience, grace, and perseverance are key as individuals navigate their way back to each other. It is through this journey of healing that individuals can discover the true power of human connection – the ability to overcome wounds, rebuild trust, and form connections that are authentic, resilient, and soulful.

In the next chapter, we will explore practical strategies and techniques that can aid in the healing process and provide guidance on how to foster soulful connections built on trust, forgiveness, and resilience.

CHAPTER XVII

The Magic of Playfulness and Laughter

Embracing Playfulness

In a world that often feels heavy and burdened, it can be all too easy to forget the importance of play. We get caught up in the responsibilities of adulthood, focusing on work, family obligations, and the countless other demands that life throws our way. But what if I told you that embracing playfulness in everyday life and relationships could be the key to unlocking a deeper sense of connection, igniting creativity, and bringing a profound sense of joy and wonder to your relationships?

It starts with a mindset shift. We must learn to embrace the childlike wonder that resides within each of us. Remember when you were a child and everything seemed magical? You saw the world through fresh eyes, finding joy in the simplest of things. As we grow older, it is easy to lose touch with that sense of wonder. However, it is not lost forever; it can be rediscovered.

One way to infuse playfulness into your everyday life is by incorporating spontaneous adventures. These could be as simple as taking a different route to work, trying a new activity with a loved one, or exploring a part of town you have never been to before. The element of surprise and spontaneity can spark a sense of excitement and joy that we often crave in our lives.

Silly games are another avenue for infusing playfulness into our relationships. Whether it's a game of charades, a round of trivia, or a playful competition, these moments of lightheartedness create memories and bonds that are lasting. Laughter becomes the glue that brings people together, fostering a deeper sense of connection and understanding.

But embracing playfulness is not just about the external activities; it is also about cultivating a playful mindset. It means being open to new experiences, allowing yourself to be vulnerable, and letting go of the need to always be serious and in control. When we let go of our inhibitions and embrace the spontaneity that playfulness brings, we open ourselves up to endless possibilities.

Research shows that playfulness has a profound impact on our well-being and relationships. It reduces stress, boosts creativity, and strengthens bonds. By infusing playfulness into our lives, we not only create a more joyful existence for ourselves but also become a beacon of light for those around us.

So, I encourage you to take a moment to reflect on your own life and relationships. Are you allowing room for playfulness? Are you allowing yourself to let go and embrace the sense of wonder that life has to offer? If not, I invite you to start small. Incorporate moments of spontaneity and silliness into your routine. Rediscover the joy of play and watch as it transforms your relationships into something truly soulful and beautiful.

The Healing Power of Laughter

To truly understand the profound impact of laughter, it is essential to delve into the science behind its magic. Research has shown that laughter triggers the release of endorphins, our body's natural feel-good hormones. These endorphins flood our system, creating an exhilarating euphoria that not only alleviates physical and emotional pain but also promotes a sense of well-being. This surge of endorphins helps reduce stress levels by lowering the production of cortisol, the notorious stress hormone that wreaks havoc on our minds and bodies. As a result, laughter becomes a source of natural therapy, fostering resilience and fortifying one's ability to cope with the challenges of life.

Beyond its physiological benefits, laughter possesses an enchanting ability to create bonds and deepen relationships. When we share moments of laughter with others, we enter into a state of synchrony, our hearts and minds aligning in perfect harmony. The infectious nature of laughter spreads like wildfire, forging unbreakable connections with those around us. Laughter's magnetic pull brings people together, dissolving barriers and strengthening the fabric of our social bonds.

Moreover, laughter brings a lightheartedness to our human encounters, removing the weight of pretense and creating a safe space for vulnerability. In moments of shared laughter, we shed our defenses and allow our authentic selves to shine through. We discover that laughter has a unique way of breaking down walls, inviting trust and fostering intimacy. It is within these moments that true connections are formed, allowing us to see and be seen in the most genuine and unfiltered way.

Cultivating laughter as a tool for connection and happiness requires a conscious effort. In our fast-paced lives filled with deadlines and responsibilities, it becomes crucial to find opportunities for humor and laughter. Surrounding ourselves with people who have a joyful disposition and a contagious sense of humor can help us tap into the healing power of laughter. Engaging in activities that bring joy and laughter, such as watching a comedy show, participating in playful games, or sharing funny anecdotes, can create a fertile ground for laughter to flourish.

It is equally important to learn to find humor in everyday situations. Life can often throw curveballs our way, but if we can train our minds to look for the funny side of things, we can transform even the most challenging moments into sources of laughter and resilience. Laughter becomes a choice, a conscious decision we make to embrace joy and create genuine connections.

As we embark on this exploration of the healing power of laughter, let us open our hearts and minds to its transformative capabilities. Let us celebrate the laughter that unifies us, that rejuvenates our spirits, and that weaves the threads of genuine connections. Through laughter, we not only nourish our own souls, but we lift others around us, creating a ripple effect of healing and happiness that touches lives far beyond our immediate surroundings.

CHAPTER XVIII

The Language of Love

Discovering Your Love Language

In my years of counseling, I have come across countless individuals who struggle in their relationships, simply because they are unaware of their primary love language. It is through this awareness that we can embark on a journey of self-discovery, unearthing the unique ways in which we express our love and long to be loved in return.

The concept of love languages was first introduced by Dr. Gary Chapman, a renowned marriage counselor, in his groundbreaking book, "The Five Love Languages: How to Express Heartfelt Commitment to Your Mate". According to Dr. Chapman, there are five primary love languages: words of affirmation, quality time, receiving gifts, acts of service, and physical touch. Each individual has a dominant love language, as well as secondary preferences, which shape how they communicate and receive love.

To embark on this journey of self-discovery, take a moment to reflect on your past and present relationships, considering which gestures and actions have made you feel truly loved and appreciated. Was it when someone showered you with words of affirmation, assuring you of your worth and significance? Or perhaps you felt the most loved when someone devoted quality time to you, fully present and engaged in the moments you shared together.

Another clue to your primary love language can be found through the ways in which you naturally express your love for others. Are you someone who enjoys giving thoughtful gifts, carefully chosen to reflect the recipient's desires and preferences? Or do you find joy in serving others, seeking to alleviate their burdens and meet their needs?

As you begin to uncover your primary love language, it is important to remember that we are not limited to expressing or receiving love solely through our dominant language. Love is a complex and multifaceted emotion, and we are capable of experiencing and understanding it through various channels. However, understanding our primary love language can greatly enhance our ability to connect deeply and authentically with others.

Once you have discovered your love language, it is essential to communicate this to your loved ones, for they cannot read your mind and intuitively know how you long to be loved. By openly sharing your preferences, you invite others to join you on this journey of love and provide them with the roadmap to your heart. Likewise, take the time to familiarize yourself with the love language of your loved ones, as this mutual understanding can foster profound intimacy and strengthen your bond.

In this pursuit of discovering our love language, we must also remain open to growth and change. Just as our preferences and needs evolve over time, so too can our love languages. It is a lifelong journey, one that allows us to continually deepen our understanding of ourselves and others.

So, my dear reader, I invite you to take a leap of faith and embark on this journey of self-discovery. Dare to uncover your primary love language and gain insights into how you prefer to give and receive love in relationships. As you navigate this terrain, remember the power that lies within you to transform your connections into soulful, genuine relationships.

Speaking the Love Language of Others

As a Christian priest and counselor, one of the most important lessons I have learned through my years of working with people is that love is not a one-size-fits-all concept. Each and every one of us has a unique way of expressing and receiving love. This is where the concept of love languages comes into play.

In my work with school and college students, as well as individuals facing various crises, I have seen firsthand the power of speaking someone's love language. It can transform relationships, cultivating deeper connections and understanding between loved ones. When we take the time to understand and adapt our communication and actions to speak the love language of others, we plant seeds of love that bear fruit in the form of harmonious relationships.

The idea of love languages was first introduced by Dr. Gary Chapman, a renowned relationship counselor and author. He identified five primary love languages: words of affirmation, quality time, acts of service, physical touch, and receiving gifts. According to Dr. Chapman, each person has a primary love language that resonates with them the most. By discovering and understanding the love language of our loved ones, we can effectively communicate love in a way that is meaningful to them.

Words of affirmation are powerful. They have the ability to build someone up or tear them down. Paying attention to the words we use can make a significant difference in our relationships. For those whose love language is words of affirmation, sincere compliments, encouraging words, and positive affirmations become the foundation of their emotional well-being. By acknowledging and affirming their worth, we show them that we care deeply for them.

Quality time is all about undivided attention and being fully present with someone. For individuals whose primary love language is quality time, meaningful conversations, shared experiences, and giving our undivided attention become the key to nurturing their souls. Disconnecting from distractions and choosing to be fully engaged with our loved ones fosters a sense of connection like no other.

Acts of service speak volumes to those who value this love language. Actions truly do speak louder than words for these individuals. Offering a helping hand, going the extra mile, and serving others selflessly are ways in which we can communicate love to them. When we take the initiative to ease their burdens or meet their needs, we show them that we value and appreciate them.

Physical touch is a powerful love language that connects us deeply with one another. A gentle touch, a loving embrace, or a simple pat on the back can communicate love to those for whom physical touch is their primary love language. But it is important to remember that physical touch should always be consensual and appropriate within the context of the relationship.

Lastly, for some, receiving gifts is the language of love. It is not about materialism or the monetary value of the gift but rather the thought and effort behind it. A well-thought-out gift that shows our understanding of their desires and interests can speak volumes to these individuals. It is a tangible way of expressing our love and appreciation for them.

In order to speak the love language of others, we must first learn to identify their primary love language. Paying attention to their words and actions can provide clues. Moreover, engaging in open and honest conversations and asking them directly can help us understand their unique love language. It is through this process of discovery that we can adapt our communication and actions to speak their language of love.

In conclusion, speaking the love language of others is a transformative practice that nurtures genuine relationships. By understanding and adapting our communication and actions to speak the love language of our loved ones, we create an environment where love can flourish. This intentional investment in the love languages of others fosters deeper connections and a greater sense of understanding. So, let us strive to love others in the way that they feel loved, empowering them to express their true selves and forging soulful connections that will withstand the test of time.

Receiving Love in Your Love Language

In my work with school and college students, as well as people going through crisis, I have noticed that many struggle with understanding and articulating their love language. They long for love and connection, but often feel unfulfilled because they are not receiving love in the way that resonates most deeply with them. This is a common issue that can hinder the growth of relationships and hinder personal growth.

It is important to explore and discover our love language, as it allows us to communicate our needs effectively to others. When we are able to clearly communicate how we receive love, we open the door for our loved ones to express their affection in a way that is meaningful to us. This can lead to a profound sense of fulfillment and connection.

To begin the journey of understanding our love language, it is essential to reflect on our own emotions and experiences. What actions or words from others make us feel loved? Is it quality time spent together? Acts of service? Words of affirmation? Receiving gifts? Physical touch? By identifying which expression of love resonates most deeply with us, we gain a clearer understanding of our own love language.

Once we have identified our love language, it is crucial to communicate this to our loved ones. Often, we expect others to instinctively know how to love us, but this is an unfair expectation. By openly sharing our love language, we give others the opportunity to express their love in a way that is specifically tailored to us.

However, communication is a two-way street. Just as we express our love language to others, we must also be open to receiving love in the way that others express their affection. This requires us to be conscientious of the love languages of those around us and to appreciate their efforts to connect with us. It may be different from our own love language, but it's important to recognize and acknowledge their expressions of love.

Receiving love in our love language is a beautiful dance of vulnerability, trust, and understanding. It requires us to be open and honest about our needs while also being willing to attune ourselves to the needs of others. Ultimately, it enhances our capacity to build genuine relationships rooted in love and connection.

CHAPTER XIX

The Power of Shared Values

Identifying Your Core Values

Reflecting on our personal values allows us to uncover the principles that have been instilled in us and continue to guide our lives. It is like peeling back the layers of our being to reveal the very foundation upon which we stand. This introspection requires us to pause, to step back from the chaos of our busy lives, and truly understand what matters most to us.

In this exploration of our values, we gain clarity on what truly drives us, inspires us, and motivates us. It is here that we discover the inherent worth and importance of our beliefs and ideals. We recognize that our values carry immense power in shaping our relationships, whether it be with our friends, family, colleagues, or even ourselves.

Our core values act as the filter through which we interpret the world around us. They guide our choices and determine how we navigate our interactions with others. When we are aligned with our values, our relationships become authentic and deeply meaningful.

Think of your values as the roots of a mighty tree, firmly planted in the fertile soil of your soul. They provide stability, grounding, and nourishment as you navigate the ever-changing landscape of relationships. Without a clear understanding of your core values, you may find yourself swayed by external influences, compromising who you truly are and what you stand for.

Take the time to reflect on your personal values. Ask yourself what truly matters to you. What principles are non-negotiable in your life? What do you hold dear and close to your heart? These questions may seem simple, but their answers hold profound insight into who you are and how you relate to others.

Once you have identified your core values, you will find that they become the guiding principles in all your relationships. They shape the way you communicate, the boundaries you set, and the level of respect and understanding you offer to others. Your values become the bedrock upon which you build your soulful connections.

Remember that everyone's core values are unique, shaped by their life experiences, culture, and personal beliefs. Embrace the diversity of values, and be open to understanding and accepting the values of others, even if they differ from your own. This acceptance and appreciation of differing values is essential in fostering genuine relationships.

As you embark on this journey of introspection and uncovering your core values, be prepared for self-discovery and growth. You may find that some values have shifted over time, while others have remained steadfast. Embrace this evolution, for it is through self-awareness and self-acceptance that we nurture and cultivate our relationships.

In conclusion, reflecting on our personal values and uncovering the principles that guide our lives is crucial to building genuine relationships. It allows us to gain clarity on what matters most to us and how our values shape our interactions with others. By understanding and honoring our core values, we create an authentic foundation upon which to connect with others in a soulful and meaningful way.

Seeking Alignment in Relationships

In my many years of working as a Christian priest and counselor, I have witnessed firsthand the transformative power of seeking alignment in relationships. It is through this process that we are able to cultivate connections that are not only genuine but also soulful. Let me share with you the wisdom and insights I have gained along the way.

The first step in seeking alignment in relationships is to recognize the significance of shared values. Values serve as guiding principles that shape our beliefs, decisions, and actions. They essentially define who we are and what we stand for. When we seek alignment in relationships, we are essentially in search of individuals whose values align with ours, creating a sense of harmony and unity.

Identifying shared values can sometimes be challenging, especially when we are meeting someone for the first time. However, there are subtle cues and indicators that can help us gauge whether there is potential for alignment. One way to do this is by engaging in open and honest conversations with others. By truly listening and observing, we can gain insight into their beliefs, opinions, and priorities. Do they prioritize compassion and empathy? Do they value honesty and integrity? These are the questions that can guide us in our search for alignment.

Fostering relationships rooted in mutual understanding and respect also requires us to be introspective. We must take the time to reflect on our own values and what we truly cherish in life. This self-awareness allows us to articulate our values to others and seek out connections with those who share similar beliefs. It is in this space of vulnerability and authenticity that genuine relationships are forged.

Furthermore, seeking alignment in relationships is an ongoing process. As we grow and evolve, our values may shift and change. It is important to have open and honest communication with the people in our lives, ensuring that our values align even as we navigate new territories. This constant commitment to seeking alignment promotes harmony and creates a fertile ground for personal growth and connection.

In closing, seeking alignment in relationships is a vital aspect of building genuine connections. When we take the time to identify shared values and foster relationships rooted in mutual understanding and respect, we create an environment where our souls can thrive. It is through this intentional search for alignment that we can build relationships that are not only fulfilling but also contribute to our overall well-being. So, let us embark on this journey together, seeking connections that touch our souls and allow us to flourish.

Nurturing a Values-Based Community

Imagine being surrounded by individuals who share your values, ideals, and aspirations. Picture a community where each person provides a sense of belonging and support. This is the essence of a values-based community. When we intentionally seek out and engage with people who resonate with our core beliefs, we create an environment that nurtures our souls and enriches our relationships.

The first step in building a values-based community is to identify and define your own values. Take the time to reflect on what truly matters to you, what guides your decisions, and what principles you hold dear. These values come from deep within your being and are the foundation upon which you will build your relationships. Once you have clarity on your values, you can actively seek out others who align with them.

To begin fostering such a community, start by engaging in activities or joining organizations that allow you to connect with like-minded individuals. Attend events or workshops that focus on topics related to your values and interests. Volunteer for causes that resonate with your heart. These are great opportunities to meet people who share similar passions and values, and who may become cherished members of your community.

In addition to seeking out new connections, it is also important to nurture the relationships you already have. Take the time to reflect on the people in your life and assess whether they align with your values. It can be difficult to distance ourselves from those who do not share our beliefs, but in order to foster a values-based community, it is essential to surround ourselves with individuals who uplift and inspire us.

Creating a values-based community does not mean that everyone has to agree on every single aspect of life. It simply means that there is a common foundation of shared values, respect, and understanding. Such a community allows for open and honest discussions, where differences are embraced and celebrated. It is within this framework that true growth and connection can occur.

When we are a part of a values-based community, we experience a profound sense of belonging. We no longer feel the need to hide or mask our true selves, as we are surrounded by individuals who accept and appreciate us for who we are. This belongingness not only nurtures our own well-being but also cultivates an environment of support and encouragement for others.

In conclusion, nurturing a values-based community is essential in building genuine and meaningful relationships. By surrounding ourselves with individuals who share our values, we create an atmosphere of belonging and support. Identify your own values, actively seek out like-minded individuals, and invest in nurturing these relationships. Embrace and celebrate differences, and remember, it is within this values-based community that your soulful connections will flourish.

CHAPTER XX

The Power of Imagination and Creativity

Unleashing Your Inner Child

In our fast-paced, adult-oriented world, it is easy to lose touch with our inner child. We become preoccupied with responsibilities, expectations, and the weight of the world on our shoulders. However, within each of us lies a treasure trove of playfulness, curiosity, and a sense of wonder waiting to be unlocked.

Embracing our inner child requires a conscious effort to let go of self-imposed limitations and stifling beliefs. We must silence our inner critic and allow our imagination to soar freely. It is through imagination that we can create new possibilities for connection in ways we never thought possible.

Once we embark on this journey of reconnecting with our inner child, we open ourselves up to the endless wonders that lie ahead. We tap into a wellspring of creativity, spontaneity, and joy. We find ourselves viewing the world with fresh eyes, discovering beauty in the smallest of details, and approaching relationships with renewed enthusiasm.

To unleash our inner child, we must first take a step back from the demands of our hectic lives. Find a quiet space, free from distractions, where you can retreat and reconnect with your authentic self. Close your eyes, take a deep breath, and allow yourself to be fully present in the moment.

As you embrace your inner child, remember the activities that brought you joy as a child. Perhaps it was playing hide and seek, building imaginary worlds with Legos, or simply sitting under a tree, lost in a book. Revisit these activities, even if it means setting aside dedicated time for them in your busy schedule. Engage in playfulness and curiosity, allowing yourself to fully immerse in the experience. Draw, dance, sing, or explore nature with the uninhibited spirit of a child.

In unleashing your inner child, it is crucial to nurture a sense of wonder. See the world through the eyes of a child, where every moment becomes an opportunity for awe and discovery. Marvel at the beauty of a blooming flower, the melody of birdsong, or the captivating colors in a vibrant sunset. Allow these moments to reignite your sense of wonder, and share them with others.

As your inner child emerges, it is important to bring this newfound energy and perspective into your relationships. Embrace the people around you with the same openness, innocence, and genuine curiosity that you display with the world. Look beyond appearances and connect with others on a soul level, allowing vulnerability and deep connection to flourish.

By reconnecting with your inner child and rediscovering the joy of imagination, you will not only enrich your own life but also nurture authentic relationships with those around you. Embrace playfulness, curiosity, and a sense of wonder, and watch as your imagination soars to create new possibilities for connection. Let the beauty of your inner child guide you on the path to building soulful connections.

The Art of Creative Expression

As a priest and counselor, I have witnessed firsthand how the power of creative expression can transform lives and strengthen relationships. In this chapter, we will delve into the various forms of creative expression such as art, music, writing, and dance, and explore how they can serve as powerful vehicles for self-expression and building connections.

In a world that often demands conformity and stifles individuality, engaging in creative activities allows us to break free from the shackles that bind us and express ourselves authentically. Whether it be with a paintbrush in hand, words flowing effortlessly from our minds onto paper, or our bodies gracefully moving in dance, creative expression grants us a limitless space for exploration and discovery.

Art, in all its forms, has the ability to convey emotions and ideas that words alone cannot capture. The strokes of a paintbrush on a canvas can communicate the inexpressible depths of sorrow or the boundless joy that fills our hearts. It allows us to transcend language barriers and reach into the core of another person's being. When we engage in artistic endeavors with others, we open the door to collaboration, shared experiences, and a deeper understanding of one another. It is through the process of creating together that we build connections that can withstand the tests of time.

Music, another powerful form of creative expression, has the ability to touch our souls in ways that words cannot. The melody and rhythm have a unique way of carrying us to a place where vulnerability and honesty reside. When we participate in music-making, whether it be through singing, playing an instrument, or simply listening intently, we are inviting others into our innermost world. The harmonious blending of voices and instruments creates a symphony of unity, where differences dissolve, and a shared experience is born. Music, indeed, has a way of making us feel as if we are part of something greater than ourselves.

Writing, too, allows us to explore the labyrinth of our thoughts and emotions. Through the art of storytelling or the pouring out of our innermost thoughts in a journal, we are able to connect with others on a profound level. When we share our written words with others, we invite them into our heartfelt experiences, granting them a glimpse into our souls. Our stories become bridges that connect us across time and space, allowing us to find common ground and understanding. By engaging in writing exercises collaboratively, we create a safe space for vulnerability and empathy, strengthening the connections we have with one another.

Lastly, dance is a form of creative expression that transcends language and cultural barriers, speaking directly to the essence of who we are. As we move our bodies in rhythm with the music, we release what is hidden in the depths of our beings. Dance is a physically embodied form of expression that communicates the stirrings of our hearts, and when we dance with others, we enter into a state of profound connection and unity. In those moments, we become part of a collective energy, where every movement becomes a word spoken without the need for verbal language.

Engaging in creative expression, be it through art, music, writing, or dance, opens up a world of possibilities for building and nurturing genuine relationships. By sharing our creative endeavors with others, we invite them into our inner world, fostering collaboration and shared experiences. So, let us embark on this journey together, as we explore the depths of our creative souls and build soulful connections that will stand the test of time.

Imagination as a Bridge

Imagine, for a moment, if you will, a world where we could truly understand and connect with each other. A world where we can bridge the gaps that separate us, and truly see the world through someone else's eyes. This is the power of using our imagination as a bridge.

Using our imagination as a bridge means being able to put ourselves in someone else's shoes, to imagine their experiences, and to foster understanding and compassion. It means going beyond our own perspective and opening our hearts and minds to the experiences of others.

The first step in using our imagination as a bridge is to cultivate empathy. Empathy is the ability to understand and share the feelings of another. It requires us to step outside of our own experiences and imagine what it must be like to walk in someone else's shoes.

To cultivate empathy, we can start by actively listening and seeking to understand others. We can ask open-ended questions and truly listen to their responses, without judgment or interruption. We can also practice reflective listening, repeating back what we hear to ensure we have understood correctly. This helps us to truly see and hear the other person, and to begin to build a bridge of understanding.

The next step is to imagine the experiences of others. Imagine what it must be like to face the challenges they have faced, to feel the emotions they have felt. This requires us to use our imagination to step into their world and see things from their perspective.

Research has shown that when we use our imagination in this way, it activates the same areas of our brain that are active when we experience the actual emotions ourselves. This allows us to truly connect with others on a deeper level, to feel what they feel, and to foster a sense of understanding and compassion.

Lastly, we must foster understanding and compassion. Understanding is the key that unlocks the door to meaningful connections. It requires us to not only imagine the experiences of others, but to also strive to understand the reasons behind their actions and behaviors. It means having an open mind and being willing to challenge our own assumptions and beliefs.

Compassion, on the other hand, is the ability to show kindness and understanding towards others, even when we may not fully understand or agree with them. It means putting ourselves in their shoes and treating them with the same love and respect we would want for ourselves.

By using our imagination as a bridge, we can transcend the limitations of our own experiences and connect with others in a deeper and more meaningful way. We can build genuine relationships based on understanding, empathy, and compassion.

So, my dear reader, I encourage you to take a moment to imagine the world through someone else's eyes. Imagine the experiences they have had, the challenges they have faced, and the emotions they have felt. Open your heart and mind to the possibilities that lie beyond your own perspective. And as you do, you will discover the true power of imagination as a bridge to connect with others on a deeper level.

CHAPTER XXI

The Art of Mindful Relationships

The Practice of Mindful Presence

Mindful presence entails the ability to let go of distractions and immerse oneself in the present moment. It requires a conscious effort to truly listen and engage with others in a deep and meaningful way. In today's fast-paced and technology-driven world, this practice has become increasingly challenging.

As we navigate through life, our minds are often consumed by a myriad of thoughts and worries. Our attention is divided, and we find it difficult to fully engage with the people around us. We are physically present, but mentally, we are preoccupied with our own inner world.

However, developing the skill of mindful presence can revolutionize our relationships. It begins with a commitment to be fully present with others, regardless of the circumstances. It means putting aside our own thoughts and distractions and giving our undivided attention to those in our presence.

One effective method for achieving mindful presence is through mindfulness techniques. Mindfulness involves intentionally paying attention to the present moment without judgment. It is about cultivating a focused awareness of our thoughts, emotions, and sensations.

In the context of relationships, mindfulness can help us let go of external distractions and focus on the person in front of us. By practicing mindfulness, we become more attuned to the nuances of their body language, the tone of their voice, and the emotions they convey. This heightened awareness enables us to respond in a more empathetic and compassionate manner, fostering a deeper connection.

Incorporating mindfulness into our daily lives can be a transformative journey. It requires practice and patience to cultivate the habit of being fully present. Simple exercises, such as mindful breathing or body scan meditations, can help train our minds to stay grounded in the present moment and silence the constant chatter of thoughts.

Additionally, setting aside dedicated time for mindful presence can be invaluable. Whether it is during a conversation with a loved one, a meeting with colleagues, or even a casual encounter with a stranger, consciously choosing to be fully present can greatly enhance the quality of our relationships.

Furthermore, the practice of mindful presence goes beyond just being physically present. It involves actively engaging with others, asking open-ended questions, and truly listening to their responses. It means suspending judgment and allowing the space for vulnerability and authenticity to flourish.

As we embark on the journey of developing mindful presence, we may encounter challenges along the way. Our minds may wander, distractions may arise, or old habits of multitasking may resurface. However, it is important to approach these obstacles with patience and self-compassion. Recognize that mindful presence is a skill that takes time to cultivate and that imperfection is a natural part of the process.

In conclusion, the practice of mindful presence is a powerful tool for building genuine relationships. By letting go of distractions, actively listening, and engaging deeply with others, we can create a space for meaningful connections to thrive. Through the use of mindfulness techniques, we can develop the skill of being fully present in our relationships, enriching our own lives and the lives of those around us.

Embracing Acceptance and Non-Judgment

Learn to cultivate acceptance and non-judgment in your relationships. Embrace others as they are, free from expectations and preconceived notions, fostering an environment of trust, understanding, and unconditional love.

When we think about building genuine relationships, it's crucial to understand the importance of acceptance and non-judgment. As a Christian priest and counselor with years of experience working with diverse groups of people, including students and individuals going through crises, I have witnessed the transformative power of embracing acceptance and letting go of judgment.

In today's world, it's all too easy to form judgments and make assumptions about others based on their outward appearance, beliefs, or actions. These preconceived notions limit our ability to truly connect with others and prevent us from discovering the beauty and depth that lies beneath the surface. If we want to build soulful connections, we must break free from our prejudices and embrace others as they are, without imposing our own expectations upon them.

But how do we do this?

Step 1: Recognize Your Own Biases

To cultivate acceptance and non-judgment, it's essential to start by examining our own biases. Our judgments often stem from the assumptions we hold or the influence of societal norms and expectations. Take a moment of honest introspection and explore the prejudices that you might unknowingly carry. It could be based on someone's ethnicity, social background, or even their appearance. Understanding our own biases is the first step toward embracing acceptance.

Step 2: Practice Empathy and Compassion

When we build relationships rooted in acceptance, we open ourselves up to the experiences and perspectives of others. Practice empathy and put yourself in the shoes of those you encounter. Seek to understand their struggles, dreams, and aspirations. By doing so, we develop a genuine sense of compassion that allows us to let go of judgment. Embracing acceptance means acknowledging and validating the experiences of others without reducing them to stereotypes or judgments based on external factors.

Step 3: Engage in Active Listening

One of the most effective ways to cultivate acceptance and non-judgment is through the art of active listening. Too often, we approach conversations with preconceived ideas and personal agendas. Instead, make a conscious effort to truly listen to the other person, without interrupting or formulating your response prematurely. By fully immersing yourself in their words and experiences, you create a safe space for them to share openly. This kind of listening not only fosters a deeper connection but also helps to eradicate judgment.

Step 4: Let Go of Expectations

Expectations can poison relationships and hinder our ability to accept others as they are. When we cling to certain expectations or try to mold someone into our idealized version of them, we undermine their essence, their uniqueness. Embracing acceptance means allowing others the freedom to express themselves authentically and without fear of judgment. Release the need for control, and instead, embrace the beauty of surprises and the unknown in each interaction.

Step 5: Foster an Environment of Trust and Unconditional Love

The ultimate goal of embracing acceptance and non-judgment is to create an environment of trust and unconditional love. When we let go of judgment, we pave the way for genuine connections to flourish. Trust emerges when we demonstrate a consistent acceptance of others, allowing them to reveal their true selves without fear of rejection. Let your relationships become a sanctuary where unconditional love flows freely, nurturing the souls of all involved.

In conclusion, embracing acceptance and non-judgment is a crucial component of building genuine relationships. By recognizing and overcoming our own biases, practicing empathy and compassion, engaging in active listening, letting go of expectations, and fostering an environment of trust and unconditional love, we can create soulful connections that transcend superficial judgments. So, let us embark on this journey of embracing acceptance and non-judgment, for it is in doing so that we unlock the true potential of our relationships and experience the transformative power of genuine connection.

Gratitude as a Nurturing Force

In this chapter, we delve into the deeply nurturing force of gratitude in building genuine relationships. As a Christian priest and counselor with years of experience working with individuals in crisis, I have witnessed firsthand the remarkable impact that gratitude can have in fostering connections and bringing about positive change. Join me on this journey as we explore the transformative power of gratitude and learn how to cultivate a sense of appreciation for the people in our lives.

Gratitude, at its core, is a profound acknowledgment of the blessings we receive from others. It is a recognition of the value, presence, and lessons that each person brings to our lives. When we cultivate a sense of gratitude, we invite humility, kindness, and compassion into our relationships. We begin to see the beauty in the small gestures, the hidden meanings behind words, and the profound impact that others have on our lives.

Expressing gratitude for the people in our lives is not merely a sign of politeness; it is a fundamental act of love and respect. It is an active choice to acknowledge and honor the role that others play in shaping our thoughts, emotions, and growth. By expressing sincere gratitude, we not only bring joy and fulfillment to those around us but also deepen our connections on a soulful level.

Research studies have shown that practicing gratitude has numerous benefits for relationships. Firstly, it enhances our sense of well-being and happiness, empowering us to approach our relationships with an open heart and a positive mindset. When we express gratitude, we focus on what is going well in our interactions with others, rather than dwelling on the challenges and shortcomings. This shift in perspective allows us to appreciate the abundance of goodness in our relationships and consequently fosters a sense of love and contentment.

Secondly, gratitude strengthens the bonds between individuals, creating a sense of belonging and connection. When we express our appreciation to others, we validate their presence and the impact they have on our lives. This validation is a powerful affirmation of their worth and builds trust, as it signals our willingness to invest time, energy, and emotional effort into the relationship. These acts of gratitude serve as nourishment to the human spirit, fostering a deep sense of belonging and emotional security.

Lastly, gratitude cultivates empathy and understanding, allowing us to see beyond our own perspective and appreciate the perspectives and experiences of others. In expressing gratitude, we acknowledge the efforts, sacrifices, and challenges that others face, revealing our capacity for empathy and compassion. This understanding creates a safe space for authentic and vulnerable communication, fostering deeper connections founded on trust and mutual respect.

To harness the transformative power of gratitude, start by pausing, reflecting, and identifying the people in your life whom you appreciate. Consider the lessons they have taught you, the moments of joy they have brought, and the ways in which they have supported you. Take the time to express your gratitude to them, whether through a heartfelt conversation, a handwritten note, or a thoughtful gesture. Remember, the act of gratitude is as much for their benefit as it is for yours.

As you cultivate a practice of gratitude, watch in awe as it deepens your connections and infuses your relationships with joy and fulfillment. Gratitude has the power to transform not only our individual lives but also the very essence of our relationships. Embraçe this awe-inspiring force and let it guide you on a journey of soulful connections, where love, respect, and appreciation become the pillars upon which genuine relationships are built.

CHAPTER XXII

The Magic of Authentic Connection

Embracing Vulnerability

In my years as a Christian priest and counselor, I have witnessed numerous individuals struggle with the concept of vulnerability. Society often teaches us to guard ourselves, to build walls and protect ourselves from the potential pain and rejection that comes with opening up. However, what we fail to realize is that by shutting off parts of ourselves, we also shut ourselves off from the possibility of genuine connections.

It was during a counseling session with a young college student named Josh that I truly understood the transformative power of vulnerability. Josh had always been an incredibly guarded individual, using sarcasm and deflection as a shield. He believed that by keeping others at arm's length, he would prevent himself from experiencing any hurt or disappointment. But it was evident to me that he longed for a deeper connection, a connection that required him to let go of his fear and embrace vulnerability.

Together, we embarked on a journey of self-discovery and growth. We began by unraveling the layers of her past and examining the experiences that had led him to build these walls around him. As we dug deeper, we discovered that Josh's fear of vulnerability stemmed from a painful betrayal in his childhood. The wounds from that experience had not healed, and he carried the burden of those scars into his adult life.

Over time, Josh began to understand that vulnerability is not a weakness, but a strength. It takes immense courage to expose our true selves to others, to risk being seen and understood. Through our counseling sessions, he learned that vulnerability is the foundation of authenticity and trust. It is through vulnerability that we can truly connect with others on a soulful level.

However, embracing vulnerability is not a solitary journey. It requires us to create a safe space for others to share their vulnerabilities as well. This concept became evident when Sarah and I organized a group therapy session for individuals facing similar struggles with vulnerability.

In this group, individuals from different walks of life came together to support one another in their journey of self-discovery. We shared our fears, struggles, and triumphs, allowing ourselves to be vulnerable in the presence of others. The bonds that were formed in that room were unlike anything I had ever witnessed before. The mutual understanding and acceptance created an environment where individuals could shed their masks and embrace their authentic selves.

Through this experience, I realized that vulnerability is not just about opening up ourselves, but also creating a space where others feel safe enough to do the same. It requires us to be compassionate listeners, without judgment or expectation. By providing this safe space, we foster an environment where genuine connections can grow and flourish.

Embracing vulnerability is a transformative journey, one that requires us to confront our fears, heal our past wounds, and step into the unknown. It is through vulnerability that we can build authentic connections, connecting not just on a superficial level, but on a deeper level of genuine understanding and acceptance. So, I invite you to embark on this journey of vulnerability, to shed your armor and open yourself up to the possibility of soulful connections.

The Power of Authentic Listening

Authentic listening, you see, is more than just a passive act of hearing. It is an intentional endeavor that requires us to be fully present and engaged, to listen with our hearts. It is about creating a sacred space where individuals can pour out their hopes, fears, and joys, knowing they will be received with compassion, empathy, and love. It is through this intentional act of genuine attention that we demonstrate our commitment to understanding and valuing others.

But what does it mean to listen with our hearts? It means setting aside our own agenda, our preconceived notions, and our desire to fix or solve. It means turning off our internal dialogue and truly immersing ourselves in the world of the other person. It means suspending judgment and truly striving to see the world through their eyes.

When we listen with our hearts, we create an environment where trust can flourish. Our undivided attention tells the other person that their thoughts and feelings matter, that they are seen and heard. It is in this sacred space of authentic listening that transformation occurs, where lives are touched, and genuine connections are built.

Imagine a young college student, burdened with the weight of expectation and uncertainty, seeking solace in my office. As I invite her to share her story, I lean in, fully present and engaged. I witness the tension in her body ease as she begins to open up, feeling the safety and acceptance in our conversation. She pours out her fears, her dreams, and her vulnerabilities, knowing that she will be seen and heard without judgment. In that moment, as tears stream down her face, I can see the immense relief wash over her. She is no longer alone, struggling silently in the depths of her own mind. She is held in the embrace of authentic listening, and it is here that she finds solace and healing.

In my years of counseling, I have witnessed countless moments like this, where the power of authentic listening has brought about profound transformation. It is not about offering solutions or advice. It is about providing a mirror for individuals to see themselves, to hear their own voices, and to rediscover their worth and significance. It is about creating a space where their truth can be brought forth, acknowledged, and held sacred.

You may be wondering how you can cultivate the art of authentic listening in your own life. It begins with a willingness to slow down, to quiet the noise within, and to be fully present in each moment. It requires vulnerability and a willingness to set aside our own ego, allowing the other person to take center stage. It means truly valuing and honoring the experiences and perspectives of others, even if they differ from our own.

As you embark on this journey of authentic listening, be prepared to be deeply moved. Prepare yourself for the profound impact of truly being seen and heard in your relationships. Authentic listening has the power to transform lives, to heal deep wounds, and to build bridges of understanding and connection. It is not a passive act, but an active choice to be present, to be engaged, and to be a vessel of love and compassion.

So let us embark on this sacred journey together, exploring the art of authentic listening and discovering the transformative power it holds. Let us create spaces of connection and understanding, where voices are heard, hearts are touched, and souls are nourished. May we be beacons of light, shining forth the gift of authentic listening in a world yearning for genuine connection.

Cultivating Mutual Understanding

We live in a world that is becoming increasingly interconnected - a global village where people from different backgrounds, cultures, and experiences coexist. In such a diverse tapestry of humanity, it is imperative that we bridge the gaps between our perspectives, cultures, and experiences. Mutual understanding allows us to do just that.

When we cultivate mutual understanding, we open ourselves up to a wealth of perspectives and experiences that may be vastly different from our own. It is through this exposure that we are able to foster empathy, compassion, and a deep sense of shared humanity. We begin to see the similarities that unite us rather than the differences that divide us.

One of the most beautiful aspects of humanity is our diversity. Each person, with their unique background and experiences, possesses a treasure trove of wisdom and insight. When we open ourselves up to understanding and celebrating this diversity, we enrich our own lives and the lives of those around us.

However, cultivating mutual understanding is not always an easy task. It requires an open mind and a willingness to step outside of our comfort zones. It calls upon us to set aside our preconceived notions and judgments and approach others with curiosity and genuine interest. It is about seeking to understand first, before seeking to be understood.

In building authentic connections, it is crucial to listen attentively and with genuine empathy. As we do so, we create a safe space for others to share their stories, their perspectives, and their emotions. We validate their experiences and honor their unique journeys. This fosters a sense of trust and emotional intimacy, which forms the bedrock of any genuine relationship.

Discovering the importance of mutual understanding is about more than just building genuine connections with others. It is about igniting a deep sense of connection with our shared humanity. It is about recognizing that, despite our differences, we are all interconnected - like threads in a tapestry, each essential to the creation of a beautiful, harmonious whole.

Remember, dear reader, that the journey towards mutual understanding is not always easy, but it is always worth it. As we embark on this exploration together, let us open our hearts and minds to the richness and beauty that lies in building authentic connections. Let us celebrate our shared humanity and strive to create a world where mutual understanding and compassion flourish.

CHAPTER XXIII

The Beauty of Synchronicity

The Power of Intuition

In today's fast-paced world, we are often bombarded with endless options and distractions, making it easy to lose sight of what truly resonates with us. However, when we learn to trust our intuition, an innate sense of knowing emerges, and we are able to navigate through the noise and chaos, finding our way to the right people and experiences.

Intuition operates on a deep, intuitive level that goes beyond our logical thinking. It is an inner knowing that arises from a place of wisdom within us, often without any rational explanation. When we tap into this intuitive power, it acts as a compass, directing us towards those individuals who are meant to be a part of our lives and vice versa.

Building soulful connections isn't just about finding people who we get along with on a surface level. It goes much deeper than that. It is about finding individuals who resonate with our essence and help us grow and evolve on our journey. These connections bring a profound sense of alignment, where the energy flows effortlessly and authentically.

Trusting our instincts and intuitions in building relationships is a skill that can be cultivated through practice and self-awareness. We learn to silence the noise of external expectations and societal pressures, and instead, turn inward to listen to the whispers of our intuition. It requires honing our ability to discern between what feels right and what doesn't, even in the absence of tangible evidence or logical reasoning.

It is important to note that intuition is not infallible. It can sometimes be clouded by our biases, fears, and anxieties. However, when we cultivate a deep sense of self-awareness, we are better equipped to differentiate between our genuine intuitive guidance and our ego's agenda. By fostering a deep connection with our inner selves, we can ensure that the choices we make in our relationships are rooted in authenticity and resonate with our core values.

Trusting our intuition in building soulful connections also requires us to be open and vulnerable. It requires us to let go of preconceived notions or expectations and embrace the unknown. Sometimes, our intuition may guide us to individuals who challenge us, push us outside our comfort zones, and help us grow in ways we never imagined. Through these connections, we learn and evolve, deepening our understanding of ourselves and others.

In a world that emphasizes superficial connections and instant gratification, cultivating soulful connections becomes even more crucial. These connections anchor us and provide a sense of belonging and purpose. They remind us that we are not alone on our journey and that there are others who share our values, dreams, and aspirations.

So, dear reader, I urge you to tap into the power of your intuition. Take a moment to listen to that inner voice, that gut feeling, that sense of knowing. Trust it, embrace it, and let it guide you towards building soulful connections. Be open to the unexpected, be receptive to the lessons that come your way, and watch as your relationships flourish with authenticity and alignment. It is through the power of intuition that the art of building genuine relationships truly comes to life.

Embracing Divine Timing

In this fast-paced world filled with instant gratification and constant busyness, it is easy to get caught up in the hustle and bustle of everyday life. We often find ourselves rushing from one task to another, always looking ahead to what is next, without taking the time to appreciate the present moment. But what if I told you that there is beauty and wisdom in slowing down and aligning ourselves with the divine timing of the universe?

The concept of divine timing reminds us that there is a greater plan at work, one that is far beyond our limited human understanding. It is the belief that everything happens for a reason, and that all events and encounters in our lives are intricately connected. When we embrace this concept, we are able to let go of our need for control and surrender ourselves to the flow of life.

Learning to be patient and trusting in the unfolding of events may at first feel challenging, especially in a world that values instant gratification and quick results. We are conditioned to believe that if we want something, we should be able to have it immediately. But true soulful connections are not forged in the realm of instant gratification; they require time, effort, and a willingness to let go of our expectations.

Patience is a virtue that is often overlooked and undervalued in today's society. But it is through patience that we allow ourselves the opportunity to grow, to learn, and to fully appreciate the journey. Just as a seed needs time to sprout and grow into a magnificent tree, relationships also need time to develop and flourish.

By surrendering to divine timing, we learn to trust in the process, knowing that everything is happening exactly as it should. We release the need to force or manipulate outcomes and instead focus on cultivating a genuine and authentic connection with ourselves and others.

When we embrace divine timing, we create space for magic to happen. We open ourselves up to unexpected synchronicities, meaningful encounters, and serendipitous events. These are the moments when the universe conspires to bring people together, weaving a tapestry of connection that is beyond our comprehension.

So, my dear reader, I implore you to take a deep breath, let go of the need for control, and surrender to the natural rhythm of life. Embrace the concept of divine timing and allow yourself to be patient and trusting. In doing so, you will find that the most magical and soulful connections are born, leading you on a path of profound growth, love, and understanding.

CHAPTER XXIV

The Art of Vulnerable Expression

The Courage to Be Seen

In a world that often encourages and rewards masks and facades, it takes great courage to break free from the molds we have created for ourselves. We construct walls, hiding behind them to shield our true selves from judgment, rejection, and the potential pain that comes with being seen. We fear that our authentic self will not be accepted, will not fit within the norms and expectations of society. Yet, it is in our vulnerability, in our willingness to show up as our true selves, that we create the space for deep connections to flourish.

To develop the courage to be seen, we must first recognize and dismantle the barriers we have built around us. These barriers are often constructed from past experiences of hurt, betrayal, or rejection. They serve as protective shields, but in doing so, they also isolate us from genuine connection. We must ask ourselves: "What am I afraid of? What am I protecting myself from?" By confronting these fears head-on, we can begin to chip away at the walls that keep us from showing up authentically.

Embracing vulnerability requires a willingness to engage in self-reflection and soul-searching. It means taking the time to explore our own emotions, fears, and insecurities, and understanding how they influence our ability to be seen. This process may involve working with a counselor or therapist who can provide guidance and support as we navigate our inner landscapes. It is through this inner work that we uncover our true selves, peeling back the layers of conditioning and societal expectations.

Once we have developed a deeper understanding of ourselves, we can then begin to share our authentic selves with others. This means being open and honest about our thoughts, feelings, and experiences, even when they may be met with discomfort or resistance. It means allowing ourselves to be seen in our fullness, embracing our imperfections and shortcomings with compassion and self-acceptance.

When we show up as our genuine selves, we create an atmosphere of trust and acceptance. Others feel seen and heard, and in turn, are more likely to show up authentically as well. Genuine connections are built on a foundation of trust, and this trust is nurtured when we have the courage to be seen. It is through vulnerability that we invite others to join us in our journey, to witness our triumphs and struggles, and to share in the joys and sorrows that life inevitably brings.

So, my dear reader, I encourage you to develop the courage to be seen in your vulnerability and embrace your authentic self. Peel back the layers of protection and step into the light of who you truly are. It is in this act of courage that you will create deep connections and cultivate relationships built on trust and acceptance. Remember, it is through showing up as our true selves that we not only find connection with others but also with our own soul.

The Healing Power of Sharing

In our society, vulnerability is often seen as a weakness, something to be avoided or hidden. We are conditioned to believe that we must maintain a façade of strength and invincibility, as showing any sign of vulnerability could expose us to judgment or rejection. But what we fail to recognize is that vulnerability is not weakness; it is courage. It takes immense strength to expose our true selves, to lay bare our struggles, fears, and insecurities in front of others.

When we choose to embrace vulnerability and share our stories, we create an invitation for others to do the same. We open up a space where genuine connections can be forged, where our shared experiences become a bridge between hearts. It is through this shared vulnerability that we begin to truly understand and empathize with one another, realizing that we are not alone in our struggles.

Research has shown that the act of sharing our experiences can have a profound impact on our emotional well-being. One study conducted at the University of California, Los Angeles, found that when participants shared their personal stories of hardship and struggle, their levels of stress and anxiety significantly decreased. Furthermore, participants reported feeling an increased sense of support and validation from those they shared with, leading to an improved sense of self-worth and belonging.

Sharing our stories not only provides us with a sense of catharsis but also allows us to gain new perspectives on our own experiences. As we listen to and empathize with the stories of others, we begin to realize that our struggles are not insurmountable, that there is hope for healing and growth. In this way, sharing becomes a two-way street, where both the storyteller and the listener can find solace and inspiration.

Therefore, it is essential that we cultivate a culture of sharing and vulnerability in our relationships, both personal and professional. We must create safe spaces where individuals feel comfortable expressing their deepest fears, insecurities, and dreams. By doing so, we allow for the healing power of connection to thrive.

It is through these soulful connections that we can truly begin to heal and grow. When we share our stories, we not only find support and understanding but also discover that we are part of something much larger than ourselves. We realize that our experiences, though unique, are universal in their human nature. And in this realization, we find solace and strength to face life's challenges head-on.

So, I invite you to explore the healing power of sharing. Open yourself up to vulnerability and embrace the courage it takes to lay bare your heart. Seek out those trusted individuals who will hold space for your stories and experiences. And in turn, be that safe haven for others, allowing them to find solace and strength in the art of shared vulnerability.

Remember, we are all connected through our shared human experience. Let us honor that connection by creating spaces where the healing power of sharing can flourish and transform lives.

The Liberation of Authentic Expression

Experience has taught me that true liberation lies in being able to express our true thoughts, feelings, and desires. It is only when we shed the mask of societal expectations and allow ourselves to be unapologetically who we are that we can truly connect with others on a deeper level. When we open ourselves up to the possibility of being truly seen and accepted, magical things can happen.

Authentic expression has the power to break down barriers and dismantle the walls we build around ourselves. When we are courageous enough to share our true thoughts and emotions, we provide others with the space to do the same. In this safe and sacred environment, genuine understanding can take root, fostering a sense of connection that transcends surface-level interaction. We create a space where vulnerability is met with empathy, and walls are no longer necessary to guard our hearts.

Reciprocity is a natural response to authentic expression. When we share our truth, we give others permission to do the same. This reciprocity forms the foundation of soulful connections. As we listen to others without judgment or expectation, we create a space for them to feel seen and heard. In turn, they are more likely to reciprocate this genuine openness, paving the way for a deep and meaningful connection. It is through this mutual vulnerability and understanding that we can build relationships that stand the test of time.

To experience the liberation that comes from authentic expression, we must be willing to peel back the layers and delve into the depths of our true selves. This requires a willingness to embrace vulnerability and confront our fears of rejection and judgment. It is a process that may feel uncomfortable at times, but the rewards far outweigh the temporary discomfort. The freedom to be ourselves and the fulfillment that comes from genuine connection are invaluable treasures that await those who dare to express their authentic selves.

In closing, I invite you to embark on a journey of self-discovery and authentic expression. Embrace the liberation that comes from speaking your truth, sharing your vulnerabilities, and allowing others to do the same. Break down the barriers, invite reciprocity, and create soulful connections founded on genuine understanding and acceptance. By doing so, you will not only transform your own relationships but also inspire others to embrace the beauty of authenticity. It is through our authenticity that we can truly connect and find the profound connection our souls crave.

CHAPTER XXV

The Joy of Giving and Receiving

The Gift of Presence

There is a profound art to building genuine relationships; one that requires us to be fully present with others. In our modern age of constant distractions and digital connectivity, it can be all too easy to overlook the power of simply being present. Yet, discovering the gift of presence and cultivating its practice can have a profound impact on our ability to forge soulful connections.

As a Christian priest and counselor, I have had the privilege of working with individuals in various stages of life, from eager school and college students to individuals grappling with crisis. Through these experiences, I have come to appreciate the transformative power of presence and its ability to foster deep connections and healing.

When we are fully present with someone, we give them our undivided attention. We set aside our own agendas, judgments, and distractions and genuinely engage with the other person. This act of being present creates a safe and sacred space where individuals can feel seen, heard, and understood.

In our fast-paced world, where multitasking has become the norm, true presence has become a rare gift. We spend so much time trying to juggle multiple tasks and demands that we often fail to give our full attention to those around us. In doing so, we miss out on the opportunities to truly connect and nurture relationships on a deeper level.

To discover the gift of presence, we must first recognize the barriers that prevent us from being truly present. One of the major obstacles is our own internal chatter, the incessant stream of thoughts that occupy our minds. We are often so wrapped up in our own concerns, judgments, and anxieties that we are unable to truly listen to others.

Additionally, our addiction to technology and constant distractions can hinder our ability to truly engage with those in front of us. We may be physically present, but our minds wander to the endless notifications, social media updates, and virtual worlds that constantly beckon our attention.

However, once we are aware of these barriers, we can begin to cultivate presence through intentional practice. One way to start is by setting aside designated times for presence, whether it be during conversations with loved ones or colleagues, or through mindfulness exercises where we focus our attention solely on the present moment.

When we practice being fully present, we create a nourishing space for genuine connection to flourish. We become attuned to the non-verbal cues, emotions, and needs of others, allowing us to respond with empathy, validation, and understanding. By setting aside our own concerns and giving our full presence, we show others that they matter, that their experiences and feelings are valid.

The impact of presence in building soulful connections cannot be overstated. When we are truly present, we not only foster deeper connections, but we also provide others with a sense of validation and appreciation. We acknowledge their worth as individuals and demonstrate our commitment to their well-being.

In my work as a counselor, I have witnessed the transformative power of presence time and time again. Through the simple act of being fully present, individuals find solace, understanding, and a renewed sense of hope. They feel seen and heard in a world that often seems indifferent and isolating.

So, I invite you to discover the gift of presence and embrace its profound impact on building soulful connections. Practice being fully present with those around you, setting aside distractions and judgments. In doing so, you will not only deepen your relationships but also contribute to a more empathetic and connected world.

The Power of Giving

Giving, in its truest form, goes beyond simply offering material possessions or financial aid. It is a mindset, a way of being in the world that seeks to uplift and support others unconditionally. When we give selflessly, we not only benefit the recipients but also experience a profound sense of fulfillment and purpose.

One of the most beautiful aspects of giving is its ability to create a ripple effect. When we extend kindness to others, it inspires them to do the same, and this chain of goodwill continues to spread throughout our networks and communities. By giving, we become part of a larger movement of positivity, creating an atmosphere of love, compassion, and unity.

In addition to the external impact, giving also deepens relationships on a personal level. When we offer our time, attention, and resources to others, we forge a connection based on empathy and understanding. It is through acts of giving that we express our care and concern for those around us, building a foundation of trust and mutual support.

Moreover, when we give selflessly, we tap into a shared sense of abundance and gratitude. Instead of approaching life from a place of scarcity and competition, generosity allows us to recognize the blessings that surround us. We acknowledge the abundance of resources, love, and opportunities available to us, and in turn, we develop a grateful heart.

Research has shown that giving can have numerous benefits for both the giver and the receiver. Studies have found that acts of kindness trigger the release of feel-good hormones in our bodies, such as dopamine and oxytocin, leading to increased happiness and reduced stress levels. Furthermore, individuals who engage in regular acts of giving report higher levels of life satisfaction and overall well-being.

As I reflect on the power of giving, I am reminded of a particular experience I had while working with college students going through a challenging time in their lives. Many of them felt isolated and overwhelmed, dealing with academic pressures, personal conflicts, and uncertainty about the future. In an effort to create a space of support and connection, I organized a community service project.

Together, we volunteered at a local homeless shelter, preparing meals and spending time with the residents. Witnessing the students' initial hesitations transform into genuine compassion and empathy was truly remarkable. The act of giving not only brought joy and hope to those in need but also allowed the students to realize the strength of their own resilience and the power of community.

Through this experience and countless others, I have seen firsthand how the power of giving can transform lives and strengthen relationships. It is not simply about giving from a place of privilege but rather about recognizing the interconnectedness of humanity and embracing our responsibility to uplift others.

In a world that often promotes self-centeredness and individual success, cultivating a spirit of giving becomes all the more essential. When we tap into the power of giving, we unlock the potential within ourselves and others to create a more compassionate and connected world. So, let us embrace the joy that comes from selfless acts of kindness and embark on a journey of building genuine relationships through the power of giving.

The Art of Receiving

To truly receive means to be vulnerable; it demands a level of trust and humility. It requires us to let go of our pride and acknowledge that we are not self-sufficient beings. We are interconnected, and our lives are enriched when we allow others to contribute to our well-being.

Learning the art of receiving starts with recognizing our own limitations. We must understand that we cannot always be the giver, the one who has all the answers, or the source of strength for others. It is okay to lean on others, seek their guidance, and accept their support. In fact, it is in receiving that we acknowledge the inherent interconnectedness of humanity.

Receiving with grace and gratitude is essential in strengthening relationships. When we accept help or kindness from others, we communicate that we trust and value their presence in our lives. We affirm their ability to contribute to our well-being, which deepens the bond between us. By allowing ourselves to receive, we create a space for others to give, fostering a sense of reciprocity in our relationships.

Receiving with grace requires humility. It means setting aside our ego and recognizing that we cannot do everything on our own. When we allow others to support us, we acknowledge that they have something valuable to offer, whether it be wisdom, compassion, or simply their presence. This act of receiving can be a transformative experience, as it opens us up to new perspectives and allows us to grow and evolve as individuals.

Gratitude is an essential component of receiving. Expressing gratitude not only acknowledges the kindness of others but also fosters a sense of appreciation and gratitude within ourselves. When we cultivate a mindset of gratitude, we become more aware of the blessings in our lives. This awareness enables us to reciprocate the love and kindness we receive, thus strengthening the relationships we cherish.

Embracing the art of receiving is an ongoing journey, one that requires patience and self-awareness. It is a delicate dance of vulnerability and trust, but it is through this dance that we can forge deep and meaningful connections with others. When we allow ourselves to receive with grace and gratitude, we break down the barriers that separate us and create space for genuine love and connection to flourish. So, let us open our hearts and embrace the beauty of receiving, for it is in this embrace that we discover the true essence of soulful connections.

CHAPTER XXVI

The Healing Power of Nature

Nature as a Source of Healing

For centuries, poets and philosophers have extolled the virtues of nature as a healing balm for the troubled soul. It is a place where the noise of the world fades into insignificance, and we can find respite from the pressures and demands of modern life. The sheer beauty of nature has a way of captivating our senses, awakening within us a sense of awe and wonder that shifts our focus away from our own worries and concerns.

But the healing power of nature is not merely a poetic notion; it has been scientifically studied and proven. Numerous research studies have shown that spending time in natural environments has a positive impact on our physical, mental, and emotional well-being. These studies have shown that immersing ourselves in nature can lower our blood pressure, reduce stress levels, improve our mood, and boost our immune system.

One particular study conducted in Japan revealed that spending just a few minutes walking in a forest can lower cortisol levels, the hormone responsible for stress. It is as if the forest gently whispers to us, soothing our anxieties and reminding us that there is a world beyond our own worries. Another study conducted by Stanford University found that spending time in nature can improve cognitive functioning and enhance our ability to focus. The natural world has a way of captivating our attention in a gentle and effortless manner, allowing our mind to rest and rejuvenate.

But the power of nature goes beyond the physical and cognitive aspects of our being. It has the ability to touch our souls, to awaken within us a sense of connectedness and belonging. When we immerse ourselves in the natural world, we become attuned to the rhythms and cycles of life, and we find solace in the knowledge that we are part of something greater than ourselves. The trees sway in harmony with the wind, the river flows with unwavering determination, and the flowers bloom with unwavering grace. In the presence of such natural beauty, we can't help but be reminded of the inherent beauty within ourselves.

Nature also serves as a reminder of our own resilience. Just as the seasons change and the flowers bloom after a long winter's slumber, so too can we find the strength and courage to rise above our own challenges. The natural world has a way of teaching us that growth and transformation are not only possible, but inevitable.

So, I invite you to step outside, to venture into the wilderness and allow nature to become your healing sanctuary. Whether it's a stroll through a nearby park, a hike in the mountains, or simply sitting under a tree in your own backyard, take the time to connect with the earth. Allow the rhythm of nature to guide you, to heal you, and to remind you of the profound interconnectedness of all things. In the embrace of nature, you will find solace, strength, and the ability to forge genuine soulful connections with both the world around you and your own self.

In the next chapter, we will delve deeper into the art of building genuine relationships and explore how these connections can play an integral role in our journey of healing and growth. But first, let us embark on this transformative exploration of nature's healing embrace.

Nature's Lessons in Connection

As I reflect upon the countless hours I have spent in nature, marveling at its beauty and mystique, I cannot help but acknowledge the invaluable lessons it has taught me about building genuine connections with others. The delicate dance of life, intertwined and harmonious, serves as a profound reminder of the interconnectedness that exists among all living beings.

In my role as a Christian priest and counselor, I have had the privilege of working with individuals facing various challenges in their lives. From school and college students grappling with the pressures of academics and identity to individuals navigating the tumultuous waters of crises, my encounters with people have reiterated the importance of establishing authentic relationships.

During my encounters with nature, I have marveled at the intricate balance and interdependence found within its ecosystems. By observing the way in which flora and fauna coexist harmoniously, I have come to understand the significance of cultivating connections built on trust, respect, and mutual support. Nature teaches us that just as each living being has its unique role to play in the ecosystem, every individual has a unique value and contribution to make in our interconnected web of relationships.

One of the most significant lessons I have learned from nature is the importance of communication. In the natural world, communication is not limited to words. Birds sing in harmonious melodies, trees sway in the breeze, and flowers attract pollinators with vibrant colors and fragrances. These nonverbal expressions teach us that communication extends beyond verbal exchanges, encouraging us to embrace various forms of expression to create deeper connections.

Moreover, nature demonstrates the significance of resilience and adaptability. Seasons change, tides rise and fall, and creatures adapt to their ever-changing environments. In the realm of relationships, the ability to navigate through ups and downs, to demonstrate resilience in the face of challenges, is paramount. Nature reminds us that genuine connections require flexibility, a willingness to adapt, and an unwavering commitment to weathering storms together.

The interconnectedness of the natural world also imparts profound lessons about the value of diversity. In nature, we witness an astonishing array of plant and animal species, each possessing unique characteristics and abilities. Similarly, in our human connections, embracing diversity strengthens the fabric of our relationships. It is through accepting and celebrating our differences that we can unlock the richness and depth of our connections with others.

In this fast-paced digital age, where virtual connections often supplant face-to-face interactions, nature serves as a timeless reminder of the immense value of genuine connections. Observing the harmonious dance of life that exists in the natural world can inspire and guide us in our endeavors to build genuine relationships. By emulating the wisdom of nature, we can learn to communicate effectively, adapt to change, embrace diversity, and foster resilient connections rooted in trust and mutual support.

As I continue to explore the profound lessons that nature teaches, I am reminded of the intricate tapestry of connections that weaves through our lives. May we all find inspiration in nature's teachings and strive to build soulful connections in our journey through life.

Nature as a Catalyst for Connection

As a priest and counselor, I have dedicated my life to helping individuals find solace and connection amidst the chaos of their lives. Over the years, I have come to understand the profound impact that nature has on our well-being and the potential it holds to deepen our relationships with others. In this chapter, we will explore how engaging in outdoor activities, such as hiking or gardening, can create opportunities for shared experiences and strengthen the bonds we have with those around us.

When we immerse ourselves in nature, something magical happens. The hustle and bustle of everyday life fades away, and we find ourselves attuned to the rhythms of the natural world. Whether it be the gentle rustle of leaves in a forest or the rhythmic crashing of waves on a beach, these simple yet profound experiences awaken a sense of awe and wonder within us. In this state of awe, we become more open, receptive, and connected to the world around us.

One of the most powerful ways to tap into this connection is through outdoor activities. Imagine embarking on a hike with a group of friends or loved ones. As you traverse the winding trails, a shared sense of adventure and excitement fills the air. Each step taken becomes a metaphor for the journey of life, and together, you conquer the challenges that come your way. Through this shared experience, a bond forms, creating a deeper understanding and appreciation for one another.

Gardening, too, offers a unique avenue for fostering connections. As you tend to a garden alongside others, you witness firsthand the transformative power of nurturing life. The camaraderie that comes from digging in the soil, planting seeds, and watching them grow is unparalleled. The act of tending to a garden requires patience, cooperation, and a shared commitment to the well-being of the plants. In this process, bonds are forged, and relationships blossom just like the flowers themselves.

Research supports the idea that nature can enhance social connections. A study conducted by the University of Illinois found that spending time in nature with others can lead to increased empathy and cooperation. In another study published in the Journal of Environmental Psychology, it was discovered that individuals who engaged in outdoor group activities reported higher levels of satisfaction and a greater sense of belonging. These findings reinforce the power of nature to bring people together and build genuine connections.

So, how can we unleash the power of nature to foster connections with others? It starts with making a conscious effort to incorporate outdoor activities into our daily lives. Organize a group hike, plan a picnic in the park, or suggest a gardening project with friends or family. By engaging in these activities, we create opportunities for shared experiences, where laughter and joy can be freely shared and memories made.

But beyond the mere act of spending time in nature, it is important to be present and mindful during these moments. Slow down, take in the sights, sounds, and smells around you. Appreciate the beauty of a flower or the majesty of a towering tree. By immersing ourselves fully in these experiences, we open the door to connection not only with nature but also with those who accompany us on this journey.

In conclusion, nature is a powerful catalyst for connection. Engaging in outdoor activities allows us to shed our inhibitions, unite in shared experiences, and deepen our relationships. Let us not underestimate the transformative effects of nature, for it has the ability to heal, inspire, and bring us closer to one another in ways that words cannot express. So, take that hike, plant that garden, and embark on the adventure of fostering true soulful connections through the embrace of nature's boundless beauty.

CHAPTER XXVII

The Magic of Rituals of Renewal

Embracing Self-Care Rituals

As a seasoned Christian priest and counselor, I have had the privilege of working with countless individuals navigating their way through various stages of life. Whether it be young students grappling with the pressures of academic success or adults going through personal crises, one thing remains constant - the importance of self-care rituals in nurturing our well-being and enhancing our ability to connect with others.

In a world plagued by busyness and constant demands, it is all too easy to neglect our own needs and prioritize the needs of others. However, soulful connections cannot be built on an empty vessel; we must first take the time to fill our own cup. Self-care rituals are like gentle reminders to ourselves that we are worthy of love and attention, that our well-being matters.

But what exactly are self-care rituals, and why are they so crucial in our pursuit of genuine relationships? Self-care rituals are practices that replenish our energy and create a strong foundation for soulful connections. They are not a luxury; they are a necessity. When we embark on the journey of embracing self-care rituals, we are ultimately giving ourselves permission to prioritize our own needs, to nurture our bodies, minds, and spirits.

The first step in embracing self-care rituals is to discover what truly nourishes us. It is a deeply personal journey, unique to each individual. Some may find solace in meditation, creating a safe space for reflection and inner peace. Others may find joy in physical activities such as yoga or hiking, allowing their bodies to move and release stress. Perhaps for you, it is indulging in a warm bubble bath, immersing yourself in a book, or spending quality time with loved ones. Whatever it may be, the key is to explore different practices and find what resonates with your soul, what fills you up from the inside out.

Once you have identified your self-care rituals, the next step is to integrate them into your daily routine. Life can often be chaotic and demanding, leaving little time for self-care. However, it is vital that we make a conscious effort to prioritize ourselves. Start small; even dedicating just a few minutes each day to self-care can make a tremendous difference in our overall well-being. Set aside specific times in your schedule for your chosen rituals, and guard them fiercely. Treat these moments as sacred, non-negotiable appointments with yourself.

As you consistently practice self-care rituals, you will start to notice a shift within yourself. Your energy will become replenished, and your ability to connect with others on a deeper level will be enhanced. Through self-care, we cultivate a strong foundation of self-love and compassion, making it easier for us to extend the same to those around us. When we are whole and nourished, we have more to give to others, and our relationships become more authentic and soulful.

In conclusion, embracing self-care rituals is an essential step on the path to building genuine relationships. It is a journey of self-discovery, of finding what truly nourishes us and prioritizing our own well-being. By integrating self-care practices into our daily lives, we create a strong foundation for soulful connections. So, I implore you, dear reader, to explore the importance of self-care and embark upon this transformative journey. May you find solace, joy, and a renewed sense of purpose as you invest in your own well-being, leading to deeper, more meaningful connections with others.

Creating Rituals of Connection

As human beings, we crave connection. We yearn for a sense of belonging, a feeling that we are an integral part of something greater than ourselves. Rituals provide us with a framework to build these connections, offering a sacred space where we can come together with loved ones and truly be present.

Take, for example, the ritual of family meals. In today's fast-paced world, it can be all too easy to prioritize individual tasks and neglect the importance of shared experiences. However, when we make the deliberate effort to gather around the table and enjoy a meal together, we are not simply fulfilling a basic need for sustenance. We are creating a ritual that signifies our commitment to the relationships within our family.

During family meals, we have the opportunity to engage in meaningful conversations and truly listen to one another. We can share stories, laughter, and sometimes even tears. Through these rituals, we build a sense of trust and understanding, deepening our connection with one another. It is within these shared moments that we can celebrate our triumphs, support one another through challenges, and create lasting memories.

Moreover, rituals can extend beyond familial relationships to encompass wider circles of connection. For instance, a weekly gathering with friends, whether it be a game night or a book club, can serve as a ritual that nourishes our friendships. By setting aside dedicated time to come together, we are reaffirming the value of these relationships. We are acknowledging that our connections with others are significant and worthy of our time and attention.

In exploring the power of shared rituals, we must also acknowledge the importance of individual rituals in our relationships. These personal rituals allow us to cultivate a deeper understanding of ourselves, which in turn enhances our ability to connect with others authentically.

For example, I recall working with a couple who were struggling to communicate effectively. They felt distant and disconnected, despite their best efforts to resolve their issues through therapy. Through our discussions, we discovered that the husband had a personal ritual of taking a solitary walk every evening. Recognizing the potential of this ritual to foster connection, I suggested that the husband invite his wife to join him on these walks.

As they began to walk side by side, hand in hand, they found solace in each other's presence. The simple act of sharing this ritual allowed them to not only enjoy the physical exercise but also to open up and engage in heartfelt conversations. Their daily walks became a safe haven, a sacred space where they could express their thoughts, fears, and dreams. Through this shared ritual, they rediscovered the depth of their love for one another and rebuilt the foundation of their relationship.

Creating rituals of connection requires intentionality and a willingness to prioritize relationships in our lives. It involves identifying activities or practices that hold personal meaning for us and consciously integrating them into our interactions with loved ones. By doing so, we honor the sacredness of our relationships and embrace the power of rituals to deepen our connections.

In the following chapters, we will delve deeper into various types of rituals that can enhance our relationships. We will explore the significance of rituals in times of crisis and how they can provide solace and strength during difficult moments. Additionally, we will examine the role of rituals in celebrating and honoring milestones, both big and small, and their power to create lasting bonds.

The art of building genuine relationships lies within the creation of rituals that allow us to connect on a soulful level. By infusing our interactions with intention, presence, and meaning, we cultivate a sense of belonging and nurture the bonds that truly matter. Let us embark on this journey of soulful connections, discovering the transformative potential of rituals in our lives.

Honoring Rituals of Transition

As human beings, we have always had a deep yearning to mark significant moments in our lives. From the moment of birth to the final breath, we have an innate desire to celebrate, honor, and navigate our transitions in a meaningful way. The art of marking these important milestones with rituals is a practice as old as time itself, and it carries with it an undeniable power to bring closure, invite new beginnings, and strengthen the bonds we share with those around us.

In our modern society, however, the significance of rituals often gets overlooked or dismissed as mere superstition. We rush through life, failing to recognize the transformative potential that rituals hold. But I firmly believe that when we become conscious of and engage in rituals with intention and reverence, we unlock a profound source of connection to our souls, one another, and the divine.

One of the most beautiful aspects of rituals is their ability to bring closure to chapters in our lives. Whether it be the end of a relationship, a change in career, or the passing of a loved one, rituals offer us an opportunity to acknowledge the pain, the grief, and the loss, and then release them, making space for healing and growth. Rituals provide a container for our emotions, allowing us to honor the past while also embracing the present and future. Through rituals, we acknowledge the importance of closure and the necessity of letting go for our own well-being.

Equally important is the role rituals play in inviting new beginnings into our lives. Just as we mark the end of a chapter, rituals provide the gateway to a fresh start. They offer us a chance to set intentions, dream big, and manifest the life we desire. When we engage in rituals that symbolize new beginnings, we invite the universe to support our aspirations and empower us on our journey. It is in these sacred moments that we plant the seeds of our future and create fertile ground for transformation and growth.

But rituals are not solely personal endeavors; they also have the power to strengthen our relationships. When we partake in rituals together, we create a shared experience that binds us in a profound and meaningful way. By honoring each other's transitions and milestones, we demonstrate our love and support for one another. Whether it be a wedding ceremony, a graduation celebration, or a retirement party, rituals provide a platform for us to come together and affirm the importance of our relationships. They remind us that we are not alone on our journey and that we have a community of loved ones standing beside us, ready to walk the path of life hand in hand.

To truly harness the power of rituals, we must be intentional in their design and execution. We must take the time to reflect on our own unique needs and desires, as well as consider the traditions and symbols that hold personal significance. It is through this intentional reflection that we lay the foundation for rituals that resonate deeply with our souls. Whether it involves crafting a simple ceremony or embracing centuries-old traditions, what matters most is the intention behind our actions.

As we embrace the power of rituals in navigating life's transitions, we honor the sacredness of our own stories and the stories of those around us. We give ourselves permission to grieve, heal, and grow. We invite new beginnings with open arms. And most importantly, we strengthen the bonds of love and connection that make our lives truly soulful. In the chapters that follow, I will guide you through the rich tapestry of ritual possibilities, offering inspiration, guidance, and practical steps to help you create meaningful rituals that honor and celebrate the transitions in your own life and the lives of those you cherish.

CHAPTER XXVIII

Conclusion: Embracing Everlasting Bonds

Renewal and Reflection

In this final chapter, we embark on a journey of renewal and reflection. For it is in these moments of introspection that we find the seeds of growth and transformation. In the hustle and bustle of our daily lives, it is easy to lose sight of what truly matters – our connections with others and the impact we have on their lives, as well as the impact they have on ours.

I encourage you to take a moment to pause and reflect on the main points we have discussed throughout this book. Firstly, we explored the importance of authenticity. Genuine relationships are built on a foundation of honesty and vulnerability. We must learn to embrace our true selves, quirks and all, for it is through this acceptance that we invite others to do the same. Authenticity cultivates trust, which forms the bedrock of lasting connections.

Next, we delved into the power of communication. Effective communication involves not just the exchange of words, but also active listening and a genuine willingness to understand others. Building genuine relationships requires us to attentively and empathetically engage with those around us, setting aside judgment and biases that may hinder mutual understanding.

Furthermore, we explored the significance of empathy and compassion. These qualities enable us to truly connect with others, allowing us to step into their shoes and experience their joys and sorrows. The ability to empathize creates a deeper level of rapport, fostering an environment where genuine relationships can flourish.

We also touched upon the importance of boundaries. Boundaries are not meant to build walls but rather to establish clear guidelines for healthy connections. It is crucial to recognize and respect the autonomy and individuality of others, while also ensuring that our own needs and emotional well-being are safeguarded.

Lastly, we delved into the art of forgiveness and the immense power it holds. Authentic relationships are not immune to disagreements and conflicts, but it is our ability to forgive and seek reconciliation that truly defines the strength of our connections. Forgiveness allows us to let go of the past and move forward, reestablishing trust and deepening the bond we share with others.

As you reflect on these main points, I hope they serve as a gentle reminder of the beauty and significance of building genuine relationships. Remember that it is not just the destination that matters but also the journey we undertake to reach it. Genuine connections are not built overnight but crafted meticulously through a series of heartfelt interactions and genuine care.

May this book serve as a guiding light on your path to building soulful connections. Embrace the lessons shared within these pages, take them to heart, and apply them to your daily interactions. The world is yearning for more genuine relationships, and you have the power to be the catalyst for change.

As I bid farewell, dear reader, I leave you with the words of Saint Francis of Assisi, a timeless reminder of the beauty and transformative power of genuine relationships: "Lord, make me an instrument of thy peace. Where there is hatred, let me sow love; where there is injury, pardon; where there is doubt, faith; where there is despair, hope; where there is darkness, light; and where there is sadness, joy."

Go forth, dear reader, and may the connections you build be soulful, genuine, and everlasting.

www.ingramcontent.com/pod-product-compliance
Lightning Source LLC
La Vergne TN
LVHW041201150826
845673LV00001B/248